Math Practice
Grades 6-7
A Best Value Book™

Written by
Kelley Wingate Levy

Edited by
Aaron Levy

© Carson-Dellosa CD-3749

ISBN 0-88724-530-7

Table of Contents

Resource Pages

The drill pages in this book are designed to evaluate a student's ability based solely on current knowledge of the material. Most drill pages, therefore, do not include explanations or examples of exercises. The following resource pages contain supplementary information relevant to the types of problems students will encounter in this book. Representative problems are broken into steps and solved, and are accompanied by descriptions of the processes involved. Students, teachers, and parents are encouraged to refer to these resource pages for instruction and clarification of concepts presented in the drill pages.

Suggestions for resource page use:
- Reproduce the resource pages and distribute to students for guidance when solving problems.
- Enlarge example problems and display them while teaching. (Alternately, post them on a bulletin board, at a work station, or in another visible area.)
- Make a transparency of problems for display on an overhead projector. Use erasable markers to review the steps for solving problems.

Included in the back of this book are removable flash cards ideal for individual review, group solving sessions, or as part of timed, sequential, or grouping activities. Carefully pull out the flash cards and cut them apart using scissors or a paper cutter.

Resource Pages

Finding Greatest Common Factor

To find the Greatest Common Factor (GCF), list all of the factors of the numbers. The factors that are the same between the numbers are the **common factors**. The number that is the highest among the common factors is the **greatest common factor**.

Example: Find the GCF for the numbers 15 and 30.

Factors of 15—1, 3, 5, (15)
Factors of 30—1, 2, 3, 5, 6, 10, (15) 30 } 1, 3, 5, and 15 are the common factors between 15 and 30. 15 is the greatest common factor.

Finding Least Common Denominator

The least common denominator (LCD) is the lowest number that 2 or more different denominators can be divided into.

Example: Find the LCD among the fractions $\frac{1}{2}$, $\frac{1}{3}$, and $\frac{1}{4}$.

Multiples of 2—2, 4, 6, 8, 10, (12)
Multiples of 3—3, 6, 9, (12)
Multiples of 4—4, 8, (12) } 12 is the least common denominator.

Fractions—Changing Fractions to Simplest Form

Change $\frac{15}{20}$ to simplest form.

1. Divide 15 and 20 by their greatest common factor, 5.

$\frac{15 \div 5}{20 \div 5} = \frac{3}{4}$

$\frac{3}{4}$ is the simplest form for $\frac{15}{20}$ because 3 and 4 have no factors in common other than 1.

Fractions—Changing Fractions to Mixed Numbers

Change $\frac{10}{7}$ to simplest form.

A fraction can be changed to a mixed number when it names a number greater than 1. This is called an improper fraction.

1. Divide 10 by 7.

$$7\overline{)10} \quad \begin{array}{r} 1\ R3 \\ \hline 10 \\ -7 \\ \hline 3 \end{array}$$

2. Since 7 goes into 10 once, the whole number will be 1. Since there is a remainder of 3, the remaining fraction is $\frac{3}{7}$. Therefore, the mixed number for $\frac{10}{7}$ is $1\frac{3}{7}$.

Fractions—Changing Mixed Numbers to Improper Fractions

Change $3\frac{1}{4}$ to simplest form.

1. Multiply the whole number, 3, by the denominator, 4.

$3 \times 4 = 12$

2. Add the numerator, 1, to 12.

$12 + 1 = 13$

3. 13 is now the new numerator. The denominator, 4, remains the same. Therefore, the improper fraction for $3\frac{1}{4}$ is $\frac{13}{4}$.

Fractions—Making Fractions Equivalent

Find a fraction equal to $\frac{1}{2}$.

To find an equivalent for a fraction, multiply the numerator and the denominator by the same number.

$\frac{1 \times 4 = 4}{2 \times 4 = 8}$ Therefore, $\frac{1}{2}$ is equal to $\frac{4}{8}$.

Fractions—Multiplying Fractions

Solve. $\frac{2}{3} \times \frac{3}{5}$

To multiply fractions, multiply the numerators and then multiply the denominators. Express answers in simplest form.

$\frac{2}{3} \times \frac{3}{5} = \frac{2 \times 3 = 6}{3 \times 5 = 15}$ Therefore, $\frac{2}{3} \times \frac{3}{5} = \frac{6}{15} = \frac{2}{5}$.

Fractions—Multiplying Whole Numbers and Fractions

Solve.	1. Rename the whole number as a fraction.	2. Multiply the fractions.
$3 \times \frac{1}{4}$	$3 = \frac{3}{1}$	$\frac{3 \times 1 = 3}{1 \times 4 = 4}$

Fractions—Multiplying Mixed Numbers and Whole Numbers

Solve.	1. Rename both the whole number and the mixed number as fractions.	2. Multiply the fractions.	3. Change to simplest form.
$3\frac{1}{5} \times 4$	$3\frac{1}{5} = \frac{16}{5} \qquad 4 = \frac{4}{1}$	$\frac{16 \times 4}{5 \times 1} = \frac{64}{5}$	$\frac{64}{5} = 12\frac{4}{5}$

Fractions—Adding Fractions with the Same Denominators

Solve.	1. Add the numerators while keeping the denominators the same.	2. Change to simplest form when possible.
$\frac{3}{8} + \frac{7}{8}$	$\frac{3+7}{8} = \frac{10}{8}$	$\frac{10}{8} = 1\frac{1}{4}$

Fractions—Adding Fractions with Different Denominators

Solve.	1. Rename the fractions so each has the same denominator.	2. Add the fractions that have been renamed.	3. Change to simplest form.
$\frac{3}{4} + \frac{2}{3}$	$\frac{3}{4} = \frac{9}{12}$ and $\frac{2}{3} = \frac{8}{12}$	$\frac{9}{12} + \frac{8}{12} = \frac{17}{12}$	$\frac{17}{12} = 1\frac{5}{12}$

Fractions—Adding Mixed Numbers with Different Denominators

Solve.	1. Rename each mixed number so that the fractions have the same denominator.	2. Rewrite the problem and solve.	3. Change to simplest form when possible.
$4\frac{3}{5} + 2\frac{1}{2}$	$4\frac{3}{5} = 4\frac{6}{10}$ and $2\frac{1}{2} = 2\frac{5}{10}$	$4\frac{6}{10} + 2\frac{5}{10} = 6\frac{11}{10}$	$6\frac{11}{10} = 7\frac{1}{10}$

Fractions—Subtracting Fractions with the Same Denominators

Solve.	1. Subtract the numerators and keep the denominators the same.	2. Change to simplest form when possible.
$\frac{5}{6} - \frac{1}{6}$	$\frac{5-1}{6} = \frac{4}{6}$	$\frac{4}{6} = \frac{2}{3}$

Fractions—Subtracting Fractions from Whole Numbers

Solve.	1. Rename the whole number so it is a fraction.	2. Rename the fractions so they have the same denominators.	3. Subtract the fractions and change to simplest form.
$8 - \frac{4}{5}$	$8 = \frac{8}{1}$	$\frac{8}{1} - \frac{4}{5} = \frac{40}{5} - \frac{4}{5}$	$\frac{40}{5} - \frac{4}{5} = \frac{36}{5} = 7\frac{1}{5}$

Fractions—Subtracting Mixed Numbers with the Same Denominators

Solve.	1. Rename $7\frac{2}{9}$ so you can subtract $3\frac{7}{9}$.	2. Use the renamed fraction to rewrite the problem.	3. Subtract the whole numbers, then subtract the fractions.
$7\frac{2}{9} - 3\frac{7}{9}$	$7\frac{2}{9} = 6 + 1\frac{2}{9} = 6\frac{11}{9}$	$6\frac{11}{9} - 3\frac{7}{9} =$	$6\frac{11}{9} - 3\frac{7}{9} = 3\frac{4}{9}$

Fractions—Subtracting Fractions with Different Denominators

Solve.
$\frac{4}{5} - \frac{2}{3}$

1. Rename the fractions so they both have the same denominator.

$$\frac{4}{5} - \frac{2}{3} = \frac{12}{15} - \frac{10}{15}$$

2. Subtract the renamed fractions.

$$\frac{12}{15} - \frac{10}{15} = \frac{2}{15}$$

Fractions—Subtracting Mixed Numbers with Different Denominators

Solve.
$4\frac{1}{2} - 2\frac{3}{7}$

1. Rename the fractions so they both have the same denominator.

$$4\frac{1}{2} = 4\frac{7}{14} \qquad 2\frac{3}{7} = 2\frac{6}{14}$$

2. Rewrite the problem with the renamed mixed numbers and subtract.

$$4\frac{7}{14} - 2\frac{6}{14} = 2\frac{1}{14}$$

Fractions—Dividing Fractions

Solve.
$\frac{1}{4} \div \frac{1}{2}$

Solve.
$8 \div \frac{1}{3}$

The multiplicative reciprocal of a number is 1 divided by the number. For example, the reciprocal of $\frac{1}{2}$ is $\frac{2}{1}$.

1. Multiply the dividend by the reciprocal of the divisor.

$$\frac{1}{4} \times \frac{2}{1} = \frac{2}{4}$$

$$\frac{8}{1} \times \frac{3}{1} = \frac{24}{1}$$

2. Simplify the fraction where possible.

$$\frac{2}{4} = \frac{1}{2}$$

$$\frac{24}{1} = 24$$

Decimals—Adding and Subtracting Decimals

Solve.
$54.03 + 3.20 =$

1. Line up the decimals and add or subtract as usual.

$$\begin{array}{r} 54.03 \\ +\ 3.20 \\ \hline 57.23 \end{array}$$

Decimals—Dividing Decimals

Solve.
$.06\overline{)5.412}$

1. Count the number of digits to the right of the decimal point in the divisor (.06).

$.06 \rightarrow$ 2 digits are to the right of the decimal.

2. Move the decimal point in the dividend (5.412) to the right as many spaces as you counted in the divisor.

$\overline{)5.41.2}$

3. Divide as usual.

$$\begin{array}{r} 90\ 2 \\ 6\overline{)541.2} \\ -54 \\ \hline 012 \\ -12 \\ \hline 0 \end{array}$$

4. Bring up the decimal point.

$$\begin{array}{r} 90.2 \\ 6\overline{)5411.2} \\ -54 \\ \hline 012 \\ -12 \\ \hline 0 \end{array}$$

Decimals—Multiplying Decimals

Solve.
$.42 \times 5.6 =$

1. Multiply as usual.

2. Count the number of digits after each decimal point in the problem and place a decimal point the same number of spaces to the left in the answer.

$$\begin{array}{r} .42 \\ \times\ 5.6 \\ \hline 2352 \end{array}$$

$.42 \longrightarrow$ 2 digits after the decimal point
$\times\ 5.6 \longrightarrow$ 1 digit after the decimal point
$2.352 \longrightarrow$ Move the decimal point three spaces to the left

Changing Decimals to Fractions

To change a decimal to a fraction, use the decimal as a numerator over either the number 10, 100, 1,000, etc. depending on the number of digits after the decimal point. Change to simplest form. Study the chart below.

Examples:

Number of digits after decimal point	1	2	3
Denominator	10	100	1,000

$$.5 = \frac{5}{10} = \frac{1}{2} \qquad .75 = \frac{75}{100} = \frac{3}{4} \qquad .125 = \frac{125}{1,000} = \frac{1}{8}$$

Changing Fractions to Decimals

To change a fraction to a decimal, divide the denominator into the numerator in the following manner.

1. If the numerator has one digit, place a decimal point just after the numerator as a dividend.

   Example: $\frac{4}{5} = 5\overline{)4.0} = .8$

2. If the numerator has two digits, place a decimal point just after the second number of the numerator as a dividend.

   Example: $\frac{25}{125} = 125\overline{)25.00} = .2$

Changing Fractions to Percentages

To change a fraction to a percentage, first change the fraction to a decimal, then multiply the decimal times 100.

Examples:

$\frac{4}{5} = 5\overline{)4.0} = .8 \qquad .8 \times 100 = 80\%$

$\frac{1}{25} = 25\overline{)1.00} = .04 \qquad .04 \times 100 = 4\%$

Changing Percentages to Fractions

To change a percentage to a fraction, multiply the percentage number times $\frac{1}{100}$ and change to simplest form.

Examples:

$75\% = 75 \times \frac{1}{100} = \frac{75}{100} = \frac{3}{4}$

$25\% = 25 \times \frac{1}{100} = \frac{25}{100} = \frac{1}{4}$

Changing Percentages to Decimals

To change a percentage to a decimal, multiply the percentage times .01.

Examples:

$7\% \times .01 = .07 \qquad 17\% \times .01 = .17 \qquad 12.5\% \times .01 = .125$

Finding Percentages

Solve.	
20% of 80 =_____	Change the percentage number to a decimal and multiply times the whole number.

20% of 80 =_____

$.20 \times 80 = 16$

Solve.	
19 is ____% of 95	Rewrite the problem in the form of an equation and solve.

1. 19 is ____% of 95
2. $19 = n\% \times 95$
3. $19 = \frac{n}{100} \times 95$
4. $19 = \frac{95n}{100}$
5. $1,900 = 95n$
6. $n = 20$

Solve.	
24 is 60% of ____	Rewrite the problem in the form of an equation and solve.

1. 24 is 60% of ____
2. $24 = \frac{60}{100} \times n$
3. $24 = \frac{60n}{100}$
4. $2,400 = 60n$
5. $n = 40$

<table>
<tr><td>

Solve.

_____ is 40% of 30

</td><td>

Rewrite the problem in the form of an equation and solve.

</td><td>

1. _____ is 40% of 30
2. $n = \frac{40}{100} \times 30$
3. $n = \frac{1200}{100}$
4. n=12

</td></tr>
</table>

Calculating Simple Interest

<table>
<tr><td>

Solve.

What is the interest for $500.00 borrowed at a rate of 12% for 2 years?

</td><td>

To calculate **simple interest**, use the following formula:
Interest = Principal ($500) x rate (12%) x time (2 years)

Interest = 500 x .12 x 2
Interest = 60 x 2
Interest = $120.00

</td></tr>
</table>

Lines, Line Segments, and Rays

A **line** is an infinite collection of points along a straight path, named by any two of its points.

A **ray** is a part of a line that infinitely extends in one direction, and is named by its endpoint and any other point.

A **line segment** is a finite part of a line, named by its two endpoints.

E   F   I   J   M   N

Parallel lines do not cross. **Perpendicular lines** cross and form right angles. **Intersecting lines** cross, but do not form right angles.

Angles

A **right angle** has a measurement of 90 degrees.

An **acute angle** has a measurement of less than 90 degrees.

An **obtuse angle** has a measurement of more than 90 degrees.

Triangles

A **right triangle** has one right angle.
An **acute triangle** has angles that are all acute.
An **obtuse triangle** has one angle that is obtuse.

right triangle   acute triangle   obtuse triangle

Finding Area of Triangles

<table>
<tr><td>

Find the area of the following triangle.

4m

6m

</td><td>

To find the area of a triangle, use the following formula:
Area = $\frac{1}{2}$ x (base x height)

Area = $\frac{1}{2}$ x (6 x 4)
Area = $\frac{1}{2}$ x 24
Area = 12 m²

</td></tr>
</table>

Finding Area of Circles

<table>
<tr><td>

Find the area of the circle.

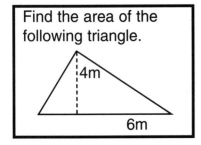

r = 2 yd

r

</td><td>

To find the area of a circle, use one of the following formulas:
Area = π x radius x radius (πr²) or Area = π x (diameter ÷ 2)²
π = 3.14
Area = π x 2 x 2
Area = π x 4
Area = 4π or 12.56 yd²

</td></tr>
</table>

Measurements—Finding Perimeter and Area

To find **perimeter**, add the length of each side of a figure.

To find the **area** of a square or rectangle, multiply the length times the width.

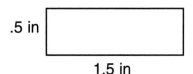

1.5 in
.5 in
.5 in
1.5 in

$1.5 + .5 + 1.5 + .5 = 4$ in

.5 in
1.5 in

$1.5 \times .5 = .75$ square in or $.75$ in^2

Finding Volume

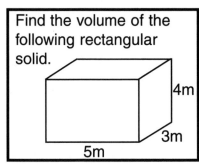

Find the volume of the following rectangular solid.

4m
3m
5m

1. Use the following formula:
   Volume = length x width x height

   Volume = 5 x 3 x 4

2. Solve the equation.

   Volume = 15 x 4
   Volume = 60 m^3

Order of Operations

Solve.

$(3 + 2) \times (7 - 1)$

The order of solving operations is as follows:
1. Calculate all math in parentheses.
2. Multiply and divide from left to right.
3. Add and subtract from left to right.

$(3 + 2) \times (7 - 1) =$
$5 \times (7 - 1) =$
$5 \times 6 =$
30

Integers

Integers include all whole numbers, both positive and negative, and the number zero.

Adding Integers

When addends have the **same sign**, add them.
   If they are both positive, the answer remains positive.
   If they are both negative, the answer is negative.
      Examples: $3 + 6 = 9$ $^-3 + {}^-6 = {}^-9$
When addends have **different signs**, subtract the numbers and use the sign of the greater addend. Examples: $^-8 + {}^+3 = {}^-5$ $^+15 + {}^-6 = 9$ $^-4 + {}^+7 = 3$ $^+3 + {}^-10 = {}^-7$

Subtracting Integers

To subtract integers, add the opposite of the number being subtracted.
      Examples: $8 - 3 = 8 + {}^-3 = 5$ $8 - {}^-3 = 8 + 3 = 11$

Calculating Exponents

To calculate a number to a certain power, multiply the root number by itself the number of times indicated by the power.
      Example:
            $2^2 = 2 \times 2 = 4$
            $2^3 = 2 \times 2 \times 2 = 8$
            $2^4 = 2 \times 2 \times 2 \times 2 = 16$
            $2^5 = 2 \times 2 \times 2 \times 2 \times 2 = 32$

Name_____

Add.

1.   42
     + 12

2.   55
     + 64

3.   83
     + 12

4.   48
     + 62

5.   55
     + 90

6.   234
     + 195

7.   558
     + 317

8.   633
     + 349

9.   458
     + 852

10.   245
     + 456

11. 5,214
     + 827

12. 1,654
     + 203

13. 3,122
     + 408

14. 3,961
     + 990

15. 4,311
     + 595

16. 1,700
     + 2,126

17. 8,909
     + 6,667

18. 4,621
     + 5,841

19. 3,031
     + 4,275

20. 6,762
     + 1,136

21. 81,037
     + 94,539

22. 32,441
     + 10,254

23. 54,622
     + 62,854

24. 40,148
     + 27,834

Total Problems 24 Problems Correct ____

1

Add.

1. $\begin{array}{r} 66 \\ + 21 \\ \hline \end{array}$
2. $\begin{array}{r} 38 \\ + 45 \\ \hline \end{array}$
3. $\begin{array}{r} 43 \\ + 28 \\ \hline \end{array}$
4. $\begin{array}{r} 74 \\ + 20 \\ \hline \end{array}$
5. $\begin{array}{r} 95 \\ + 89 \\ \hline \end{array}$

6. $\begin{array}{r} 185 \\ + 122 \\ \hline \end{array}$
7. $\begin{array}{r} 399 \\ + 421 \\ \hline \end{array}$
8. $\begin{array}{r} 159 \\ + 179 \\ \hline \end{array}$
9. $\begin{array}{r} 128 \\ + 397 \\ \hline \end{array}$
10. $\begin{array}{r} 742 \\ + 325 \\ \hline \end{array}$

11. $\begin{array}{r} 1,214 \\ + \ 854 \\ \hline \end{array}$
12. $\begin{array}{r} 4,781 \\ + \ 125 \\ \hline \end{array}$
13. $\begin{array}{r} 3,214 \\ + \ 285 \\ \hline \end{array}$
14. $\begin{array}{r} 2,325 \\ + \ 456 \\ \hline \end{array}$
15. $\begin{array}{r} 7,951 \\ + \ 351 \\ \hline \end{array}$

16. $\begin{array}{r} 1,780 \\ + 4,522 \\ \hline \end{array}$
17. $\begin{array}{r} 7,919 \\ + 6,328 \\ \hline \end{array}$
18. $\begin{array}{r} 2,852 \\ + 3,122 \\ \hline \end{array}$
19. $\begin{array}{r} 3,188 \\ + 4,357 \\ \hline \end{array}$
20. $\begin{array}{r} 6,851 \\ + 1,111 \\ \hline \end{array}$

21. $\begin{array}{r} 81,037 \\ + 23,539 \\ \hline \end{array}$
22. $\begin{array}{r} 62,264 \\ + 13,142 \\ \hline \end{array}$
23. $\begin{array}{r} 75,421 \\ + 72,840 \\ \hline \end{array}$
24. $\begin{array}{r} 49,122 \\ + 87,834 \\ \hline \end{array}$

Total Problems _24_ Problems Correct ____

Add.

1.	584	2.	560	3.	385	4.	882	5.	541
	845		884		256		456		241
	+ 217		+ 551		+ 382		+ 127		+ 369

6.	2,456	7.	3,570	8.	4,687	9.	5,285	10.	3,221
	8,445		2,869		4,258		1,124		4,654
	+ 2,778		+ 2,210		+ 6,621		+ 5,038		+ 6,213

11.	40,554	12.	69,721	13.	4,349	14.	21,254	15.	68,695
	5,654		21,065		88		51,342		3,072
	+ 3,122		+ 2,985		+ 524		+ 852		+ 210

16.	47,107	17.	5,045	18.	5,840	19.	2,215	20.	8,841
	52,001		622		636		782		654
	42,932		18		59		560		9,388
	+ 207		+ 5		+ 2,129		+ 49		+ 78

Total Problems __20__ Problems Correct ____

Skill: Subtracting Two and Three Digit Numbers

Subtract.

1.	451 − 35	2.	588 − 22	3.	358 − 62	4.	535 − 23	5.	525 − 78

6.	147 − 65	7.	325 − 58	8.	352 − 21	9.	817 − 24	10.	622 − 45

11.	467 − 457	12.	865 − 255	13.	921 − 650	14.	885 − 214	15.	841 − 562

16.	951 − 123	17.	725 − 582	18.	540 − 185	19.	806 − 652	20.	885 − 504

21.	721 − 129	22.	784 − 694	23.	456 − 283	24.	345 − 116	25.	668 − 422

Total Problems _25_ Problems Correct ____

Name_____   Skill: Subtracting Two, Three, Four, Five,
                                         and Six Digit Numbers

Subtract.

1. 6,567   2. 6,232   3. 8,421   4. 9,219   5. 1,359
   –   52   –   25   –   88   –   85   –   28

6. 5,487   7. 5,512   8. 7,247   9. 8,824   10. 5,427
   – 225   – 808   – 448   – 488   – 131

11. 45,107   12. 51,257   13. 46,687   14. 52,399   15. 56,571
   – 3,458   – 4,071   – 5,674   – 1,008   – 6,221

16. 86,961   17. 87,810   18. 35,300   19. 96,127
   – 71,831   – 52,516   – 28,704   – 73,279

20. 472,175   21. 566,502   22. 227,645   23. 517,523
   – 68,189   – 10,498   – 53,217   – 46,211

Total Problems 23   Problems Correct ____

Name **Lora**

Multiply.

1. 52
    x 48
    416
    +2080
    2496

2. 75
    x 52
    150
    +3750
    3,900

3. 43
    x 71
    43
    +3010
    3053

4. 62
    x 82
    124
    +4960
    5,084

5. 35
    x 17
    245
    +350
    595

6. 21 ✓
    x 11
    21
    +21
    231

7. 98 ✓
    x 93
    274
    +882
    9,094

8. 31 ✓
    x 41
    31
    +124
    1,271

9. 77
    x 65
    385
    +462
    5,005

10. 45
    x 50
    00
    225
    2250

11. 84 ✓
    x 21
    84
    +1680
    1,764

12. 22
    x 17
    154
    +220
    374

13. 47 ✓
    x 38
    376
    +1,410
    1,786

14. 48 ✓
    x 52
    96
    +2400
    2496

15. 98 ✓
    x 40
    00
    +392
    3,920

16. 685 ✓
    x 21
    685
    +13700
    14,385

17. 322 ✓
    x 23
    966
    +644
    7,406

18. 724 ✓
    x 43
    2172
    +2896
    31,132

19. 518
    x 59
    4662
    +11900
    16,562

20. 42 ✓
    x 57
    294
    +210
    3394

Lora's major problem seemed to be adding her answers incorrectly. She made 6 one multiplication error on #19.

Total Problems 20 Problems Correct 14

6

Name_____

Multiply.

1. 23
  x 45

2. 85
  x 61

3. 22
  x 12

4. 87
  x 56

5. 34
  x 22

6. 41
  x 35

7. 62
  x 51

8. 39
  x 49

9. 88
  x 25

10. 33
  x 12

11. 21
  x 31

12. 48
  x 62

13. 38
  x 22

14. 39
  x 54

15. 90
  x 12

16. 225
  x 17

17. 854
  x 56

18. 885
  x 95

19. 369
  x 84

20. 215
  x 66

Total Problems 20   Problems Correct ____

Name_____   Skill: Multiplying Two, Three, and Four
                                         Digit Numbers

Multiply.

1. 885×62

2. 558×31

3. 668×51

4. 830×95

5. 741×51

6. 611×231

7. 729×106

8. 147×535

9. 844×462

10. 512×787

11. 818×500

12. 271×235

13. 682×623

14. 431×638

15. 335×213

16. $8,242 \times 682$

17. $3,851 \times 492$

18. $4,341 \times 863$

19. $7,433 \times 682$

20. 892×214

Total Problems 20   Problems Correct ____

Name_____   Skill: Dividing by One Digit Numbers

Divide.

1. $8\overline{)64}$ 2. $9\overline{)81}$ 3. $7\overline{)42}$ 4. $8\overline{)56}$ 5. $6\overline{)24}$

6. $5\overline{)25}$ 7. $8\overline{)24}$ 8. $6\overline{)54}$ 9. $8\overline{)16}$ 10. $9\overline{)90}$

11. $6\overline{)30}$ 12. $7\overline{)77}$ 13. $6\overline{)36}$ 14. $5\overline{)35}$ 15. $9\overline{)63}$

16. $5\overline{)40}$ 17. $8\overline{)32}$ 18. $3\overline{)12}$ 19. $7\overline{)14}$ 20. $6\overline{)60}$

21. $4\overline{)20}$ 22. $9\overline{)27}$ 23. $5\overline{)30}$ 24. $9\overline{)36}$ 25. $9\overline{)63}$

Total Problems 25 Problems Correct ____

Name_____   Skill: Dividing by Two Digit Numbers

Divide.

1. $22\overline{)308}$ 2. $11\overline{)286}$ 3. $16\overline{)832}$ 4. $41\overline{)574}$

5. $17\overline{)306}$ 6. $33\overline{)957}$ 7. $53\overline{)901}$ 8. $62\overline{)744}$

9. $24\overline{)1,200}$ 10. $38\overline{)1,064}$ 11. $45\overline{)1,485}$ 12. $57\overline{)3,591}$

13. $86\overline{)4,730}$ 14. $74\overline{)3,848}$ 15. $91\overline{)5,096}$ 16. $18\overline{)1,296}$

17. $73\overline{)4,453}$ 18. $29\overline{)1,798}$ 19. $82\overline{)1,968}$ 20. $95\overline{)3,990}$

Total Problems __20__ Problems Correct ____

Name __June 5__   Skill: Changing Fractions to Simplest Form

Change each fraction or mixed number to simplest form.

1. $\dfrac{6}{8} = \dfrac{3}{4}$ 2. $\dfrac{2}{4} = \dfrac{1}{2}$ 3. $\dfrac{15}{18} = \dfrac{5}{6}$ 4. $\dfrac{16}{24} = \dfrac{2}{3}$ 5. $\dfrac{10}{40} = \dfrac{1}{4}$

6. $\dfrac{6}{15} = \dfrac{2}{5}$ 7. $\dfrac{2}{10} = \dfrac{1}{5}$ 8. $\dfrac{20}{40} = \dfrac{1}{2}$ 9. $\dfrac{16}{32} = \dfrac{1}{2}$ 10. $\dfrac{56}{64} = \dfrac{7}{8}$

11. $\dfrac{27}{81} = \dfrac{3}{9} \quad \dfrac{1}{3}$ 12. $\dfrac{12}{24} = \dfrac{1}{2}$ 13. $\dfrac{10}{15} = \dfrac{2}{3}$ 14. $\dfrac{14}{21} = \dfrac{2}{3}$ 15. $\dfrac{25}{30} = \dfrac{5}{6}$

16. $2\dfrac{24}{30} = 2\dfrac{4}{5}$ 17. $3\dfrac{12}{18} = 3\dfrac{6}{8} \; 3\dfrac{3}{4} \quad 3\dfrac{2}{3}$ 18. $1\dfrac{18}{20} = 1\dfrac{9}{10}$ 19. $4\dfrac{3}{24} = 4\dfrac{1}{8}$

20. $4\dfrac{4}{8} = 4\dfrac{1}{2}$ 21. $5\dfrac{10}{15} = 5\dfrac{2}{3}$ 22. $3\dfrac{6}{9} = 3\dfrac{2}{3}$ 23. $2\dfrac{8}{32} = 2\dfrac{1}{4}$

Total Problems __23__   Problems Correct __22__

Change each fraction or mixed number to simplest form.

1. $\dfrac{4}{8} =$ 2. $\dfrac{2}{8} =$ 3. $\dfrac{15}{21} =$ 4. $\dfrac{16}{20} =$ 5. $\dfrac{10}{60} =$

6. $\dfrac{4}{16} =$ 7. $\dfrac{3}{12} =$ 8. $\dfrac{30}{40} =$ 9. $\dfrac{12}{32} =$ 10. $\dfrac{49}{63} =$

11. $\dfrac{28}{70} =$ 12. $\dfrac{13}{39} =$ 13. $\dfrac{12}{15} =$ 14. $\dfrac{18}{36} =$ 15. $\dfrac{9}{9} =$

16. $1\dfrac{36}{48} =$ 17. $3\dfrac{15}{30} =$ 18. $2\dfrac{18}{20} =$ 19. $6\dfrac{3}{12} =$

20. $5\dfrac{3}{9} =$ 21. $4\dfrac{12}{15} =$ 22. $5\dfrac{7}{7} =$ 23. $4\dfrac{9}{36} =$

Total Problems _23_ Problems Correct ____

Change each mixed number to a fraction.

1. $2\frac{5}{8} =$

2. $4\frac{1}{2} =$

3. $6\frac{3}{4} =$

4. $3\frac{6}{7} =$

5. $8\frac{7}{8} =$

6. $2\frac{1}{9} =$

7. $8\frac{5}{11} =$

8. $3\frac{3}{10} =$

9. $4\frac{5}{12} =$

10. $8\frac{2}{3} =$

11. $2\frac{3}{5} =$

12. $5\frac{5}{7} =$

Total Problems __12__ Problems Correct ____

Change each mixed number to a fraction.

1. $3\frac{5}{9} =$

2. $3\frac{1}{3} =$

3. $5\frac{2}{4} =$

4. $5\frac{6}{8} =$

5. $7\frac{3}{5} =$

6. $4\frac{1}{6} =$

7. $7\frac{4}{10} =$

8. $2\frac{7}{11} =$

9. $1\frac{6}{12} =$

10. $5\frac{2}{3} =$

11. $7\frac{3}{5} =$

12. $3\frac{5}{7} =$

Total Problems __12__ Problems Correct ____

Change each fraction to a mixed number.

1. $\dfrac{13}{7} =$

2. $\dfrac{10}{6} =$

3. $\dfrac{32}{7} =$

4. $\dfrac{21}{16} =$

5. $\dfrac{37}{14} =$

6. $\dfrac{55}{19} =$

7. $\dfrac{12}{5} =$

8. $\dfrac{14}{13} =$

9. $\dfrac{50}{21} =$

10. $\dfrac{43}{20} =$

Total Problems 10 Problems Correct ____

Change each fraction to a mixed number.

1. $\dfrac{13}{5}$ =

2. $\dfrac{12}{5}$ =

3. $\dfrac{32}{7}$ =

4. $\dfrac{48}{17}$ =

5. $\dfrac{36}{11}$ =

6. $\dfrac{77}{20}$ =

7. $\dfrac{13}{4}$ =

8. $\dfrac{15}{12}$ =

9. $\dfrac{30}{21}$ =

10. $\dfrac{53}{22}$ =

Total Problems _10_ Problems Correct ____

Name_____

Find the least common denominator for each pair of fractions.

1. $\dfrac{1}{6}, \dfrac{2}{5}$ _____

2. $\dfrac{1}{6}, \dfrac{3}{5}$ _____

3. $\dfrac{2}{4}, \dfrac{1}{7}$ _____

4. $\dfrac{1}{9}, \dfrac{2}{2}$ _____

5. $\dfrac{3}{5}, \dfrac{3}{8}$ _____

6. $\dfrac{2}{5}, \dfrac{1}{2}$ _____

7. $\dfrac{1}{2}, \dfrac{3}{5}$ _____

8. $\dfrac{5}{8}, \dfrac{3}{9}$ _____

9. $\dfrac{3}{7}, \dfrac{1}{2}$ _____

10. $\dfrac{7}{5}, \dfrac{2}{6}$ _____

11. $\dfrac{3}{7}, \dfrac{1}{9}$ _____

12. $\dfrac{1}{5}, \dfrac{1}{3}$ _____

Total Problems _12_ Problems Correct ____

Add. Write answers in simplest form.

1. $\dfrac{1}{4} + \dfrac{2}{4} =$

2. $\dfrac{1}{5} + \dfrac{2}{5} =$

3. $\dfrac{1}{6} + \dfrac{3}{6} =$

4. $\dfrac{1}{9} + \dfrac{2}{9} =$

5. $\dfrac{3}{8} + \dfrac{7}{8} =$

6. $\dfrac{7}{11} + \dfrac{1}{11} =$

7. $\dfrac{3}{6} + \dfrac{2}{6} =$

8. $\dfrac{5}{9} + \dfrac{8}{9} =$

9. $\dfrac{1}{2} + \dfrac{1}{2} =$

10. $\dfrac{2}{7} + \dfrac{4}{7} =$

11. $\dfrac{7}{12} + \dfrac{2}{12} =$

12. $\dfrac{2}{5} + \dfrac{5}{5} =$

13. $\dfrac{5}{15} + \dfrac{2}{15} =$

14. $\dfrac{9}{13} + \dfrac{8}{13} =$

15. $\dfrac{9}{17} + \dfrac{8}{17} =$

Total Problems __15__ Problems Correct ____

Name_____

Add. Write answers in simplest form.

1. $\dfrac{1}{7}$
    $+ \ \dfrac{2}{7}$

2. $\dfrac{1}{3}$
    $+ \ \dfrac{2}{3}$

3. $\dfrac{4}{12}$
    $+ \ \dfrac{5}{12}$

4. $\dfrac{6}{10}$
    $+ \ \dfrac{7}{10}$

5. $\dfrac{4}{6}$
    $+ \ \dfrac{1}{6}$

6. $\dfrac{2}{7}$
    $+ \ \dfrac{1}{7}$

7. $\dfrac{3}{15}$
    $+ \ \dfrac{3}{15}$

8. $\dfrac{8}{11}$
    $+ \ \dfrac{6}{11}$

9. $\dfrac{5}{8}$
    $+ \ \dfrac{1}{8}$

10. $\dfrac{1}{3}$
    $+ \ \dfrac{2}{3}$

11. $\dfrac{2}{15}$
    $+ \ \dfrac{4}{15}$

12. $\dfrac{4}{10}$
    $+ \ \dfrac{2}{10}$

13. $\dfrac{4}{9}$
    $+ \ \dfrac{2}{9}$

14. $\dfrac{10}{17}$
    $+ \ \dfrac{11}{17}$

15. $\dfrac{5}{18}$
    $+ \ \dfrac{3}{18}$

16. $\dfrac{1}{2}$
    $+ \ \dfrac{1}{2}$

Total Problems 16 Problems Correct ____

19

Add. Write answers in simplest form.

1. $\dfrac{1}{2} + \dfrac{2}{5} =$

2. $\dfrac{2}{3} + \dfrac{3}{5} =$

3. $\dfrac{1}{4} + \dfrac{3}{8} =$

4. $\dfrac{1}{6} + \dfrac{3}{4} =$

5. $\dfrac{3}{7} + \dfrac{1}{3} =$

6. $\dfrac{1}{10} + \dfrac{2}{20} =$

7. $\dfrac{1}{8} + \dfrac{3}{4} =$

8. $\dfrac{1}{9} + \dfrac{2}{7} =$

9. $\dfrac{2}{5} + \dfrac{1}{3} =$

10. $\dfrac{2}{3} + \dfrac{3}{4} =$

11. $\dfrac{7}{10} + \dfrac{3}{12} =$

12. $\dfrac{2}{5} + \dfrac{5}{6} =$

13. $\dfrac{5}{12} + \dfrac{2}{10} =$

14. $\dfrac{1}{6} + \dfrac{3}{5} =$

15. $\dfrac{1}{4} + \dfrac{2}{7} =$

Total Problems 15 Problems Correct ____

Name_____

Skill: Adding Fractions with Different Denominators

Add. Write answers in simplest form.

1.
$$\frac{1}{4}$$
$$+\ \frac{3}{5}$$

2.
$$\frac{4}{5}$$
$$+\ \frac{7}{8}$$

3.
$$\frac{3}{6}$$
$$+\ \frac{3}{4}$$

4.
$$\frac{1}{3}$$
$$+\ \frac{5}{7}$$

5.
$$\frac{1}{2}$$
$$+\ \frac{1}{5}$$

6.
$$\frac{2}{3}$$
$$+\ \frac{5}{6}$$

7.
$$\frac{1}{4}$$
$$+\ \frac{2}{3}$$

8.
$$\frac{1}{3}$$
$$+\ \frac{7}{8}$$

9.
$$\frac{4}{5}$$
$$+\ \frac{2}{3}$$

10.
$$\frac{3}{4}$$
$$+\ \frac{1}{3}$$

11.
$$\frac{5}{8}$$
$$+\ \frac{2}{3}$$

12.
$$\frac{2}{3}$$
$$+\ \frac{2}{10}$$

13.
$$\frac{2}{3}$$
$$+\ \frac{2}{5}$$

14.
$$\frac{1}{6}$$
$$+\ \frac{2}{5}$$

15.
$$\frac{2}{5}$$
$$+\ \frac{1}{3}$$

16.
$$\frac{2}{7}$$
$$+\ \frac{2}{3}$$

Total Problems 16   Problems Correct ____

© Carson-Dellosa CD-3749

21

Name_____   Skill: Adding Mixed Numbers

Add. Write answers in simplest form.

1. $4\frac{1}{8} + 5\frac{3}{4} =$

2. $6\frac{1}{2} + 6\frac{2}{5} =$

3. $3\frac{1}{9} + 2\frac{1}{3} =$

4. $4\frac{7}{8} + 6\frac{1}{4} =$

5. $8\frac{1}{3} + 2\frac{3}{7} =$

6. $5\frac{2}{3} + 7\frac{3}{7} =$

7. $4\frac{3}{4} + 1\frac{2}{3} =$

8. $5\frac{1}{8} + 6\frac{2}{5} =$

9. $2\frac{5}{6} + 3\frac{1}{3} =$

10. $4\frac{1}{8} + 5\frac{1}{5} =$

11. $1\frac{9}{10} + 3\frac{1}{4} =$

12. $5\frac{1}{2} + 6\frac{2}{7} =$

13. $8\frac{3}{4} + 7\frac{3}{16} =$

14. $2\frac{3}{4} + 3\frac{5}{6} =$

15. $1\frac{3}{8} + 1\frac{1}{4} =$

Total Problems __15__ Problems Correct ____

Name_____

Add. Write answers in simplest form.

1. $5\frac{1}{6} + 2\frac{3}{4} =$

2. $3\frac{1}{3} + 4\frac{2}{5} =$

3. $1\frac{1}{7} + 8\frac{1}{5} =$

4. $4\frac{7}{8} + 6\frac{1}{3} =$

5. $8\frac{1}{2} + 2\frac{3}{7} =$

6. $5\frac{2}{8} + 7\frac{3}{7} =$

7. $2\frac{3}{4} + 1\frac{2}{3} =$

8. $7\frac{1}{8} + 5\frac{2}{5} =$

9. $1\frac{5}{6} + 3\frac{1}{3} =$

10. $3\frac{1}{8} + 5\frac{1}{6} =$

11. $4\frac{9}{10} + 3\frac{1}{5} =$

12. $5\frac{1}{4} + 6\frac{2}{7} =$

13. $8\frac{3}{4} + 7\frac{3}{13} =$

14. $2\frac{3}{5} + 3\frac{5}{6} =$

15. $1\frac{3}{8} + 1\frac{1}{2} =$

Total Problems 15   Problems Correct ____

Name_____

Subtract. Write answers in simplest form.

1. $\dfrac{5}{6} - \dfrac{1}{6} =$

2. $\dfrac{7}{8} - \dfrac{3}{8} =$

3. $\dfrac{3}{10} - \dfrac{1}{10} =$

4. $\dfrac{15}{16} - \dfrac{7}{16} =$

5. $\dfrac{3}{4} - \dfrac{1}{4} =$

6. $\dfrac{5}{7} - \dfrac{2}{7} =$

7. $\dfrac{7}{9} - \dfrac{1}{9} =$

8. $\dfrac{4}{5} - \dfrac{2}{5} =$

9. $\dfrac{5}{9} - \dfrac{2}{9} =$

10. $\dfrac{5}{8} - \dfrac{1}{8} =$

11. $\dfrac{2}{3} - \dfrac{1}{3} =$

12. $\dfrac{3}{6} - \dfrac{2}{6} =$

13. $\dfrac{7}{8} - \dfrac{5}{8} =$

14. $\dfrac{5}{9} - \dfrac{4}{9} =$

15. $\dfrac{5}{7} - \dfrac{3}{7} =$

16. $\dfrac{2}{5} - \dfrac{1}{5} =$

17. $\dfrac{3}{7} - \dfrac{2}{7} =$

18. $\dfrac{4}{6} - \dfrac{2}{6} =$

19. $\dfrac{2}{3} - \dfrac{1}{3} =$

20. $\dfrac{3}{4} - \dfrac{2}{4} =$

Total Problems __20__ Problems Correct ____

Name_____

Subtract. Write answers in simplest form.

1. $\dfrac{2}{5} - \dfrac{1}{5} =$

2. $\dfrac{7}{8} - \dfrac{3}{8} =$

3. $\dfrac{7}{10} - \dfrac{3}{10} =$

4. $\dfrac{11}{14} - \dfrac{9}{14} =$

5. $\dfrac{5}{7} - \dfrac{2}{7} =$

6. $\dfrac{2}{3} - \dfrac{1}{3} =$

7. $\dfrac{7}{8} - \dfrac{5}{8} =$

8. $\dfrac{5}{6} - \dfrac{1}{6} =$

9. $\dfrac{3}{5} - \dfrac{1}{5} =$

10. $\dfrac{7}{9} - \dfrac{5}{9} =$

11. $\dfrac{2}{3} - \dfrac{1}{3} =$

12. $\dfrac{4}{5} - \dfrac{2}{5} =$

13. $\dfrac{2}{8} - \dfrac{1}{8} =$

14. $\dfrac{4}{6} - \dfrac{1}{6} =$

15. $\dfrac{5}{9} - \dfrac{1}{9} =$

16. $\dfrac{1}{2} - \dfrac{1}{2} =$

17. $\dfrac{2}{4} - \dfrac{1}{4} =$

18. $\dfrac{4}{7} - \dfrac{2}{7} =$

19. $\dfrac{4}{8} - \dfrac{1}{8} =$

20. $\dfrac{3}{5} - \dfrac{2}{5} =$

Total Problems 20 Problems Correct ____

Name_____

Subtract. Write answers in simplest form.

1. $\frac{3}{9}$
    $-\frac{1}{4}$

2. $\frac{2}{3}$
    $-\frac{4}{9}$

3. $\frac{7}{12}$
    $-\frac{1}{4}$

4. $\frac{2}{3}$
    $-\frac{1}{2}$

5. $\frac{5}{6}$
    $-\frac{1}{5}$

6. $\frac{3}{4}$
    $-\frac{1}{5}$

7. $\frac{2}{6}$
    $-\frac{2}{8}$

8. $\frac{3}{9}$
    $-\frac{1}{4}$

9. $\frac{1}{2}$
    $-\frac{1}{4}$

10. $\frac{7}{8}$
    $-\frac{3}{10}$

11. $\frac{9}{10}$
    $-\frac{1}{2}$

12. $\frac{2}{4}$
    $-\frac{1}{3}$

13. $\frac{7}{8}$
    $-\frac{1}{9}$

14. $\frac{1}{3}$
    $-\frac{1}{6}$

15. $\frac{1}{5}$
    $-\frac{1}{8}$

16. $\frac{5}{7}$
    $-\frac{2}{9}$

17. $\frac{1}{5}$
    $-\frac{1}{8}$

18. $\frac{8}{8}$
    $-\frac{4}{6}$

19. $\frac{8}{9}$
    $-\frac{3}{6}$

20. $\frac{6}{6}$
    $-\frac{3}{12}$

Total Problems 20   Problems Correct ____

Subtract. Write answers in simplest form.

1. $\dfrac{3}{4}$
   $-\dfrac{1}{6}$

2. $\dfrac{5}{6}$
   $-\dfrac{2}{5}$

3. $\dfrac{11}{12}$
   $-\dfrac{1}{6}$

4. $\dfrac{5}{12}$
   $-\dfrac{1}{3}$

5. $\dfrac{3}{4}$
   $-\dfrac{1}{3}$

6. $\dfrac{13}{15}$
   $-\dfrac{2}{3}$

7. $\dfrac{2}{3}$
   $-\dfrac{1}{6}$

8. $\dfrac{5}{6}$
   $-\dfrac{3}{7}$

9. $\dfrac{7}{8}$
   $-\dfrac{1}{6}$

10. $\dfrac{8}{9}$
    $-\dfrac{5}{6}$

11. $\dfrac{2}{3}$
    $-\dfrac{7}{12}$

12. $\dfrac{11}{14}$
    $-\dfrac{1}{2}$

13. $\dfrac{7}{8}$
    $-\dfrac{1}{9}$

14. $\dfrac{1}{3}$
    $-\dfrac{1}{6}$

15. $\dfrac{3}{12}$
    $-\dfrac{1}{10}$

16. $\dfrac{5}{6}$
    $-\dfrac{1}{3}$

17. $\dfrac{7}{12}$
    $-\dfrac{1}{4}$

18. $\dfrac{7}{8}$
    $-\dfrac{1}{2}$

19. $\dfrac{2}{3}$
    $-\dfrac{4}{9}$

20. $\dfrac{5}{6}$
    $-\dfrac{1}{8}$

Total Problems __20__ Problems Correct ____

Subtract. Write answers in simplest form.

1.
$$2 - \frac{7}{8}$$

2.
$$4 - \frac{2}{5}$$

3.
$$5 - \frac{2}{3}$$

4.
$$6 - \frac{1}{8}$$

5.
$$3 - \frac{3}{4}$$

6.
$$8 - \frac{9}{10}$$

7.
$$7 - \frac{4}{5}$$

8.
$$4 - \frac{3}{10}$$

9.
$$5 - \frac{6}{9}$$

10.
$$4 - \frac{2}{6}$$

11.
$$5 - \frac{2}{5}$$

12.
$$10 - \frac{1}{2}$$

13.
$$12 - \frac{5}{7}$$

14.
$$9 - \frac{1}{3}$$

15.
$$4 - \frac{7}{8}$$

16.
$$3 - \frac{6}{7}$$

Total Problems 16   Problems Correct ____

Name_____

Subtract. Write answers in simplest form.

1.
$$15 - \frac{3}{8}$$

2.
$$10 - \frac{2}{5}$$

3.
$$1 - \frac{1}{3}$$

4.
$$2 - \frac{6}{11}$$

5.
$$5 - \frac{3}{5}$$

6.
$$9 - \frac{3}{7}$$

7.
$$14 - \frac{2}{9}$$

8.
$$13 - \frac{2}{3}$$

9.
$$1 - \frac{7}{8}$$

10.
$$6 - \frac{1}{5}$$

11.
$$7 - \frac{5}{6}$$

12.
$$5 - \frac{1}{4}$$

13.
$$8 - \frac{3}{4}$$

14.
$$4 - \frac{1}{2}$$

15.
$$2 - \frac{1}{6}$$

16.
$$6 - \frac{3}{7}$$

Total Problems __16__ Problems Correct ____

Name_____   Skill: Subtracting Mixed Numbers with the
                                         Same Denominators

Subtract.

1. $8\frac{4}{5}$
    $-1\frac{1}{5}$

2. $5\frac{2}{3}$
    $-4\frac{1}{3}$

3. $3\frac{1}{2}$
    $-1\frac{1}{2}$

4. $4\frac{2}{6}$
    $-3\frac{5}{6}$

5. $5\frac{3}{12}$
    $-2\frac{2}{12}$

6. $3\frac{3}{5}$
    $-1\frac{4}{5}$

7. $10\frac{1}{4}$
    $-7\frac{1}{4}$

8. $6\frac{7}{8}$
    $-1\frac{1}{8}$

9. $5\frac{1}{3}$
    $-4\frac{2}{3}$

10. $5\frac{3}{8}$
    $-3\frac{3}{8}$

11. $9\frac{6}{7}$
    $-2\frac{2}{7}$

12. $2\frac{1}{8}$
    $-1\frac{1}{8}$

13. $7\frac{3}{8}$
    $-5\frac{1}{8}$

14. $4\frac{11}{13}$
    $-2\frac{12}{13}$

15. $7\frac{1}{6}$
    $-5\frac{3}{6}$

16. $3\frac{7}{9}$
    $-2\frac{1}{9}$

Total Problems _16_ Problems Correct ____

30

Name_____   Skill: Subtracting Mixed Numbers with the
                                                              Same Denominators

Subtract. Change answers to simplest form.

1. $12\frac{7}{8}$ 2. $10\frac{2}{5}$ 3. $6\frac{1}{6}$ 4. $2\frac{2}{3}$
    $-\ 5\frac{5}{8}$ $-\ 7\frac{4}{5}$ $-\ 5\frac{5}{6}$ $-\ 1\frac{1}{3}$

5. $3\frac{1}{4}$ 6. $8\frac{7}{10}$ 7. $4\frac{5}{6}$ 8. $9\frac{7}{12}$
    $-\ 2\frac{3}{4}$ $-\ 7\frac{9}{10}$ $-\ 2\frac{1}{6}$ $-\ 4\frac{5}{12}$

9. $10\frac{2}{3}$ 10. $8\frac{1}{2}$ 11. $8\frac{3}{16}$ 12. $4\frac{11}{18}$
    $-\ 9\frac{1}{3}$ $-\ 6\frac{1}{2}$ $-\ 7\frac{5}{16}$ $-\ 1\frac{13}{18}$

13. $3\frac{1}{8}$ 14. $5\frac{12}{16}$ 15. $6\frac{1}{9}$ 16. $8\frac{7}{10}$
    $-\ 1\frac{7}{8}$ $-\ 5\frac{12}{16}$ $-\ 2\frac{3}{9}$ $-\ 6\frac{3}{10}$

Total Problems __16__   Problems Correct ____

31

Name_____

Multiply. Change answers to simplest form.

1. $\dfrac{3}{6} \times \dfrac{2}{3} =$

2. $\dfrac{1}{7} \times \dfrac{5}{5} =$

3. $\dfrac{5}{7} \times \dfrac{4}{6} =$

4. $\dfrac{1}{2} \times \dfrac{3}{4} =$

5. $\dfrac{2}{5} \times \dfrac{4}{6} =$

6. $\dfrac{4}{9} \times \dfrac{3}{7} =$

7. $\dfrac{3}{6} \times \dfrac{3}{4} =$

8. $\dfrac{3}{9} \times \dfrac{2}{4} =$

9. $\dfrac{2}{5} \times \dfrac{3}{5} =$

10. $\dfrac{2}{6} \times \dfrac{5}{8} =$

11. $\dfrac{1}{6} \times \dfrac{3}{8} =$

12. $\dfrac{4}{6} \times \dfrac{2}{3} =$

13. $\dfrac{3}{5} \times \dfrac{6}{8} =$

14. $\dfrac{2}{3} \times \dfrac{4}{7} =$

15. $\dfrac{7}{9} \times \dfrac{3}{4} =$

Total Problems __15__ Problems Correct ____

Multiply. Change answers to simplest form.

1. $\frac{3}{5}$ x $\frac{2}{6}$ =

2. $\frac{2}{4}$ x $\frac{3}{7}$ =

3. $\frac{1}{9}$ x $\frac{3}{6}$ =

4. $\frac{3}{9}$ x $\frac{2}{5}$ =

5. $\frac{3}{8}$ x $\frac{5}{6}$ =

6. $\frac{4}{7}$ x $\frac{3}{8}$ =

7. $\frac{4}{6}$ x $\frac{2}{5}$ =

8. $\frac{3}{4}$ x $\frac{2}{3}$ =

9. $\frac{2}{5}$ x $\frac{6}{8}$ =

10. $\frac{2}{4}$ x $\frac{1}{6}$ =

11. $\frac{3}{5}$ x $\frac{7}{8}$ =

12. $\frac{1}{4}$ x $\frac{1}{5}$ =

13. $\frac{2}{7}$ x $\frac{4}{5}$ =

14. $\frac{3}{6}$ x $\frac{1}{6}$ =

15. $\frac{1}{3}$ x $\frac{4}{7}$ =

Total Problems __15__ Problems Correct ____

Multiply. Write answers in simplest form.

1. $5 \times \dfrac{2}{5} =$

2. $\dfrac{2}{3} \times 4 =$

3. $\dfrac{3}{4} \times 5 =$

4. $8 \times \dfrac{1}{7} =$

5. $\dfrac{1}{9} \times 6 =$

6. $2 \times \dfrac{4}{5} =$

7. $6 \times \dfrac{3}{8} =$

8. $\dfrac{5}{6} \times 4 =$

9. $\dfrac{2}{7} \times 6 =$

10. $4 \times \dfrac{8}{9} =$

11. $\dfrac{4}{6} \times 3 =$

12. $7 \times \dfrac{3}{5} =$

13. $2 \times \dfrac{3}{7} =$

14. $\dfrac{4}{5} \times 6 =$

15. $7 \times \dfrac{5}{6} =$

Total Problems 15 Problems Correct ____

Multiply. Change answers to simplest form.

1. $4 \times \frac{1}{2} =$ 2. $\frac{2}{5} \times 3 =$ 3. $\frac{1}{3} \times 7 =$

4. $2 \times \frac{2}{5} =$ 5. $\frac{1}{8} \times 5 =$ 6. $4 \times \frac{3}{4} =$

7. $4 \times \frac{2}{7} =$ 8. $\frac{5}{7} \times 5 =$ 9. $\frac{6}{8} \times 2 =$

10. $3 \times \frac{5}{6} =$ 11. $\frac{2}{3} \times 2 =$ 12. $5 \times \frac{4}{5} =$

13. $8 \times \frac{1}{8} =$ 14. $\frac{3}{9} \times 4 =$ 15. $3 \times \frac{2}{3} =$

Total Problems _15_ Problems Correct ____

Name_____

Multiply. Change answers to simplest form.

1. $4 \times 3\frac{3}{5} =$

2. $10 \times 5\frac{1}{2} =$

3. $2 \times 5\frac{1}{8} =$

4. $6 \times 9\frac{4}{5} =$

5. $8 \times 2\frac{3}{8} =$

6. $3 \times 1\frac{15}{16} =$

7. $2 \times 8\frac{3}{4} =$

8. $5 \times 4\frac{2}{5} =$

9. $4 \times 8\frac{6}{7} =$

10. $9 \times 1\frac{1}{18} =$

11. $2 \times 7\frac{5}{8} =$

12. $2 \times 2\frac{1}{4} =$

Total Problems _12_ Problems Correct ____

Name_____   Skill: Multiplying Mixed Numbers
                                                      and Whole Numbers

Multiply. Change answers to simplest form.

1. $2 \times 2\frac{1}{3} =$

2. $4 \times 5\frac{1}{8} =$

3. $7 \times 1\frac{3}{4} =$

4. $3 \times 5\frac{1}{5} =$

5. $6 \times 3\frac{1}{6} =$

6. $7 \times 2\frac{3}{5} =$

7. $9 \times 3\frac{2}{3} =$

8. $5 \times 6\frac{5}{8} =$

9. $4 \times 2\frac{1}{2} =$

10. $8 \times 9\frac{1}{10} =$

11. $3 \times 9\frac{1}{3} =$

12. $7 \times 2\frac{1}{7} =$

Total Problems __12__ Problems Correct ____

Name_____   Skill: Dividing Fractions

Divide. Write answers in simplest form.

1. $\dfrac{3}{4} \div \dfrac{5}{6} =$ 2. $\dfrac{3}{16} \div \dfrac{3}{8} =$ 3. $\dfrac{7}{9} \div \dfrac{2}{3} =$

4. $\dfrac{5}{8} \div \dfrac{3}{5} =$ 5. $\dfrac{4}{9} \div \dfrac{3}{4} =$ 6. $\dfrac{7}{8} \div \dfrac{5}{11} =$

7. $\dfrac{7}{10} \div \dfrac{3}{5} =$ 8. $\dfrac{7}{8} \div \dfrac{2}{3} =$ 9. $\dfrac{2}{5} \div \dfrac{3}{8} =$

10. $\dfrac{4}{7} \div \dfrac{3}{7} =$ 11. $\dfrac{1}{6} \div \dfrac{4}{5} =$ 12. $\dfrac{2}{3} \div \dfrac{4}{5} =$

13. $\dfrac{3}{5} \div \dfrac{7}{8} =$ 14. $\dfrac{3}{4} \div \dfrac{3}{5} =$ 15. $\dfrac{9}{16} \div \dfrac{3}{4} =$

Total Problems _15_ Problems Correct ____

Name_____

Divide. Write answers in simplest form.

1. $\dfrac{1}{2} \div \dfrac{7}{8} =$

2. $\dfrac{6}{11} \div \dfrac{3}{8} =$

3. $\dfrac{7}{9} \div \dfrac{2}{5} =$

4. $\dfrac{5}{6} \div \dfrac{1}{5} =$

5. $\dfrac{3}{4} \div \dfrac{3}{4} =$

6. $\dfrac{7}{8} \div \dfrac{5}{12} =$

7. $\dfrac{7}{13} \div \dfrac{4}{5} =$

8. $\dfrac{11}{12} \div \dfrac{2}{9} =$

9. $\dfrac{2}{3} \div \dfrac{3}{8} =$

10. $\dfrac{4}{7} \div \dfrac{4}{5} =$

11. $\dfrac{1}{8} \div \dfrac{3}{5} =$

12. $\dfrac{2}{5} \div \dfrac{2}{7} =$

13. $\dfrac{3}{8} \div \dfrac{5}{9} =$

14. $\dfrac{1}{4} \div \dfrac{3}{7} =$

15. $\dfrac{9}{17} \div \dfrac{1}{4} =$

Total Problems __15__ Problems Correct ____

Name_____

Divide. Write answers in simplest form.

1. $8 \div \dfrac{6}{7} =$

2. $\dfrac{5}{6} \div 10 =$

3. $\dfrac{2}{5} \div 3 =$

4. $3 \div \dfrac{1}{2} =$

5. $\dfrac{2}{3} \div 6 =$

6. $10 \div \dfrac{6}{7} =$

7. $12 \div \dfrac{3}{4} =$

8. $\dfrac{3}{4} \div 4 =$

9. $\dfrac{4}{7} \div 5 =$

10. $14 \div \dfrac{7}{8} =$

11. $\dfrac{1}{2} \div 6 =$

12. $6 \div \dfrac{1}{5} =$

13. $8 \div \dfrac{1}{2} =$

14. $\dfrac{1}{4} \div 2 =$

15. $9 \div \dfrac{1}{3} =$

Total Problems 15 Problems Correct ____

Name_____

Divide. Write answers in simplest form.

1. $5 \div \frac{6}{8} =$

2. $\frac{5}{5} \div 12 =$

3. $\frac{2}{3} \div 3 =$

4. $2 \div \frac{3}{7} =$

5. $\frac{2}{5} \div 3 =$

6. $8 \div \frac{3}{5} =$

7. $6 \div \frac{5}{6} =$

8. $\frac{3}{8} \div 3 =$

9. $\frac{4}{5} \div 2 =$

10. $12 \div \frac{1}{2} =$

11. $\frac{1}{2} \div 5 =$

12. $5 \div \frac{1}{5} =$

13. $3 \div \frac{1}{6} =$

14. $\frac{1}{4} \div 4 =$

15. $8 \div \frac{1}{3} =$

Total Problems 15 Problems Correct ____

Name_____

Divide. Write answers in simplest form.

1. $1\frac{1}{6} \div \frac{1}{4} =$

2. $2\frac{3}{4} \div \frac{1}{8} =$

3. $6\frac{1}{8} \div \frac{4}{7} =$

4. $3\frac{1}{4} \div \frac{3}{8} =$

5. $2\frac{1}{2} \div \frac{1}{2} =$

6. $2\frac{3}{4} \div \frac{1}{2} =$

7. $5\frac{2}{3} \div \frac{9}{10} =$

8. $2\frac{1}{4} \div \frac{3}{8} =$

9. $1\frac{1}{4} \div \frac{2}{3} =$

10. $1\frac{4}{5} \div \frac{2}{7} =$

11. $4\frac{1}{2} \div \frac{1}{2} =$

12. $1\frac{2}{5} \div \frac{1}{3} =$

Total Problems _12_ Problems Correct ____

Divide. Write answers in simplest form.

1. $1\frac{1}{6} \div \frac{1}{4} =$

2. $3\frac{1}{2} \div \frac{1}{4} =$

3. $1\frac{1}{3} \div \frac{3}{8} =$

4. $2\frac{2}{5} \div \frac{2}{3} =$

5. $5\frac{1}{3} \div \frac{3}{8} =$

6. $3\frac{3}{5} \div 10 =$

7. $6\frac{3}{8} \div \frac{7}{10} =$

8. $3\frac{1}{3} \div \frac{3}{4} =$

9. $1\frac{1}{5} \div \frac{2}{5} =$

10. $1\frac{1}{3} \div \frac{7}{8} =$

11. $2\frac{1}{3} \div 5 =$

12. $5\frac{6}{7} \div \frac{3}{4} =$

Total Problems _12_ Problems Correct ____

Name_____

Make the following fractions equivalent.

1. $\dfrac{1}{2} = \dfrac{}{4}$ 2. $\dfrac{3}{4} = \dfrac{}{12}$ 3. $\dfrac{1}{4} = \dfrac{}{8}$ 4. $\dfrac{1}{3} = \dfrac{3}{}$ 5. $\dfrac{2}{5} = \dfrac{6}{}$

6. $\dfrac{3}{5} = \dfrac{}{20}$ 7. $\dfrac{2}{3} = \dfrac{}{12}$ 8. $\dfrac{2}{7} = \dfrac{4}{}$ 9. $\dfrac{2}{3} = \dfrac{6}{}$ 10. $\dfrac{3}{4} = \dfrac{9}{}$

11. $\dfrac{5}{6} = \dfrac{}{42}$ 12. $\dfrac{1}{5} = \dfrac{}{25}$ 13. $\dfrac{3}{7} = \dfrac{}{28}$ 14. $\dfrac{1}{8} = \dfrac{8}{}$ 15. $\dfrac{1}{6} = \dfrac{5}{}$

Complete each row to make each fraction equal to the first one.

16. $\dfrac{1}{2} = \dfrac{}{6} = \dfrac{4}{} = \dfrac{}{12} = \dfrac{2}{} = \dfrac{}{10}$

17. $\dfrac{2}{3} = \dfrac{}{12} = \dfrac{4}{} = \dfrac{}{15} = \dfrac{6}{} = \dfrac{}{18}$

18. $\dfrac{1}{4} = \dfrac{}{8} = \dfrac{5}{} = \dfrac{}{12} = \dfrac{6}{} = \dfrac{}{16}$

19. $\dfrac{3}{5} = \dfrac{}{25} = \dfrac{9}{} = \dfrac{}{10} = \dfrac{12}{} = \dfrac{}{30}$

Total Problems __19__ Problems Correct ____

Add.

1. 2.4
    + 1.7

2. 8.1
    + 9.2

3. 10.3
    + 7.4

4. 1.5
    + 1.5

5. 18.6
    + 9.5

6. 14.3
    + 1.9

7. 24.7
    + 32.6

8. 20.5
    + 32.3

9. .01
    + .72

10. 1.04
    + 2.07

11. 16.52
    + 13.63

12. 14.87
    + 56.09

13. 3.2
    1.4
    + 7.8

14. 86.7
    5.2
    + 8.4

15. 9.1
    12.5
    + 19.4

16. 40.08
    60.27
    + 50.33

17. 2.016
    3.094
    + 8.627

18. 42.65
    87.61
    + 12.12

19. 492.6
    382.3
    + 225.7

20. 4.008
    1.318
    + .056

Total Problems 20 Problems Correct ____

45

Name_____

Add.

1.   2.34
      .02
  + 1.65

2. 22.87
    45.7
  + 1.26

3.   .605
    1.70
  + 23.75

4.   .2
     1.2
   + .12

5. 543.7
     3.42
  +   .06

6. 987.5
     1.4
  + 30.2

7. 86.15
     .07
  + 5.72

8.   1.45
    20.03
  +   .17

9. 72.56
    12.38
  +   .07

10. 2.14
      .007
   + 72.4

11.   5.1
     7.53
   + 87.4

12.   4.5
      5.4
   + 12.67

13. 42.7 + .03 + 1.7 =

14. .725 + 1.33 + 12 =

15. 87.5 + 1.2 + 591.35 =

16. 42 + .543 + 7.8 =

Total Problems __16__ Problems Correct ____

Name_____

Subtract.

1. 19.867   2. 20.342   3. 1.428   4. 32.456
   – 1.070   – .67   – 1.2   – 1.2

5. 4.52   6. 756.83   7. 71.34   8. 81.384
   – .4   – 22.5   – 2.672   – 2.777

9. 4.254   10. 38.7   11. 31.1   12. 24.75
   – 3.01   – 5.21   – 3.052   – 6.243

13. $23.154 - 3.08 =$ 14. $.65 - .224 =$

15. $.7 - .506 =$ 16. $2.3 - 1.437 =$

Total Problems __16__ Problems Correct ____

Name_____   Skill: Subtracting Decimals

Subtract.

1.
```
   .8
 − .3
```

2.
```
   .9
 − .4
```

3.
```
   .3
 − .2
```

4.
```
   .6
 − .2
```

5.
```
   .47
 − .21
```

6.
```
   .27
 − .25
```

7.
```
   .22
 − .15
```

8.
```
   .40
 − .11
```

9.
```
   .741
 − .215
```

10.
```
   .833
 − .501
```

11.
```
   .428
 − .338
```

12.
```
   .575
 − .104
```

13.
```
   4.6
 − 2.1
```

14.
```
   3.6
 − .2
```

15.
```
   39.6
 − .7
```

16.
```
   36.06
 − 3.72
```

17.
```
   40.15
 − .22
```

18.
```
   86.33
 − 6.21
```

19.
```
   85.43
 − 15.07
```

20.
```
   52.27
 − 5.41
```

Total Problems __20__ Problems Correct ____

Name_____ Skill: Multiplying Decimals

Multiply.

1. .2
    x 3

2. .9
    x 3

3. .2
    x .1

4. .6
    x .8

5. .08
    x 6

6. .04
    x 5

7. 6
    x .12

8. 5
    x .25

9. 5.7
    x 6

10. 4.3
    x 2

11. 1.07
    x 6

12. 2.15
    x .8

13. .14
    x .27

14. 7.2
    x 5.3

15. .04
    x .06

16. 1.3
    x 3.1

17. .67
    x 5.4

18. 7.1
    x 5.5

19. .07
    x 15

20. 32
    x 6.4

Total Problems 20 Problems Correct ____

49

Name_____   Skill: Multiplying Decimals

Multiply.

1. .256
    x 1.3

2. 9.42
    x 3.3

3. 2.41
    x .8

4. 5.11
    x .64

5. .121
    x 110

6. 43.7
    x 12.5

7. 15.2
    x 14.7

8. 8.12
    x .732

9. .908
    x .402

10. 121.5
    x 54.7

11. 60.45
    x 7.26

12. 3.225
    x .36

13. 37.556 x 23.4 =

14. .612 x 5.37 =

15. 3.729 x 438.7 =

16. 34.4 x .002 =

Total Problems __16__ Problems Correct ____

Name_____ Skill: Dividing Decimals

Divide.

1. $8\overline{)4.8}$ 2. $4\overline{)5.2}$ 3. $3\overline{)2.1}$ 4. $5\overline{).25}$ 5. $4\overline{)3.2}$

6. $6\overline{)2.4}$ 7. $8\overline{).72}$ 8. $5\overline{).30}$ 9. $3\overline{).12}$ 10. $4\overline{)4.4}$

11. $4\overline{).20}$ 12. $8\overline{).32}$ 13. $.02\overline{)26}$ 14. $.7\overline{)49}$ 15. $.03\overline{)30}$

16. $.6\overline{)42}$ 17. $.08\overline{)2.4}$ 18. $.5\overline{)5.0}$ 19. $.2\overline{).20}$ 20. $.4\overline{)2.3}$

Total Problems __20__ Problems Correct ____

Name_____   Skill: Dividing Decimals

Divide.

1. $4\overline{)3.2}$ 2. $.12\overline{)48}$ 3. $.3\overline{)12}$ 4. $.04\overline{)1.25}$

5. $.3\overline{)3.03}$ 6. $2.2\overline{)1.32}$ 7. $3\overline{).303}$ 8. $4\overline{)25.2}$

9. $15\overline{)30.30}$ 10. $1.2\overline{)1.20}$ 11. $.35\overline{)700}$ 12. $.5\overline{)15.55}$

13. $1.9\overline{)4.37}$ 14. $.06\overline{).600}$ 15. $5.1\overline{)38.25}$ 16. $5.7\overline{)35.34}$

Total Problems __16__ Problems Correct ____

Name_____   Skill: Changing Fractions and Mixed
                                                 Numbers to Decimals

Change the following fractions or mixed numbers to decimals.

1. $\frac{1}{4}$ =   2. $\frac{2}{5}$ =   3. $\frac{49}{50}$ =   4. $\frac{17}{10}$ =   5. $\frac{1}{5}$ =

6. $\frac{7}{50}$ =   7. $\frac{2}{10}$ =   8. $\frac{31}{50}$ =   9. $\frac{13}{50}$ =   10. $\frac{9}{10}$ =

11. $\frac{3}{5}$ =   12. $\frac{3}{4}$ =   13. $\frac{7}{20}$ =   14. $\frac{7}{25}$ =   15. $\frac{3}{10}$ =

16. $1\frac{2}{5}$ =   17. $3\frac{31}{50}$ =   18. $1\frac{43}{50}$ =   19. $4\frac{4}{25}$ =

20. $4\frac{4}{8}$ =   21. $5\frac{1}{5}$ =   22. $4\frac{1}{4}$ =   23. $2\frac{8}{32}$ =

Total Problems 23   Problems Correct ____

53

Change the following fractions or mixed numbers to decimals.

1. $\dfrac{3}{5}$ =

2. $\dfrac{3}{10}$ =

3. $\dfrac{3}{6}$ =

4. $\dfrac{4}{5}$ =

5. $\dfrac{1}{8}$ =

6. $\dfrac{1}{10}$ =

7. $\dfrac{7}{8}$ =

8. $\dfrac{11}{20}$ =

9. $\dfrac{2}{8}$ =

10. $\dfrac{12}{25}$ =

11. $\dfrac{1}{4}$ =

12. $\dfrac{11}{25}$ =

13. $5\dfrac{6}{12}$ =

14. $4\dfrac{12}{24}$ =

15. $1\dfrac{4}{5}$ =

16. $5\dfrac{2}{5}$ =

17. $4\dfrac{15}{30}$ =

18. $6\dfrac{7}{8}$ =

Total Problems _18_ Problems Correct ____

Change each decimal to a fraction. Change to simplest form when possible.

1. .25 =

2. .05 =

3. .12 =

4. .88 =

5. .015 =

6. .250 =

7. .02 =

8. .15 =

9. .75 =

10. .35 =

11. .125 =

12. .825 =

13. .18 =

14. .60 =

15. .20 =

16. .225 =

Total Problems _16_ Problems Correct ____

Name_____ Skill: Changing Decimals to Fractions

Change each decimal to a fraction or mixed number.

1. .008 =

2. .018 =

3. .921 =

4. .4 =

5. .45 =

6. .16 =

7. .155 =

8. .032 =

9. 2.2 =

10. 4.05 =

11. 4.62 =

12. 6.25 =

13. 3.024 =

14. .12 =

15. .018 =

16. 3.25 =

Total Problems __16__ Problems Correct ____

Name_____   Skill: Changing Percentages to Fractions

Change the percentages to fractions. Change to simplest form when possible.

1. **20% =**

2. **25% =**

3. **30% =**

4. **50% =**

5. **75% =**

6. **22% =**

7. **10% =**

8. **4% =**

9. **15% =**

10. **80% =**

11. **27% =**

12. **200% =**

13. **31% =**

14. **125% =**

15. **85% =**

16. **175% =**

Total Problems __16__ Problems Correct _____

Name_____ Skill: Changing Percentages to Fractions

Change the percentages to fractions. Change to simplest form when possible.

1. **44% =**

2. **88% =**

3. **25% =**

4. **80% =**

5. **65% =**

6. **78% =**

7. **24% =**

8. **42% =**

9. **10% =**

10. **18% =**

11. **45% =**

12. **70% =**

13. **56% =**

14. **15% =**

15. **11% =**

16. **120% =**

Total Problems _16_ Problems Correct ____

Name_____   Skill: Changing Percentages to Fractions

Change the percentages to fractions. Change to simplest form when possible.

1. **144%** =

2. **65%** =

3. **38%** =

4. **55%** =

5. **25%** =

6. **32%** =

7. **12%** =

8. **42%** =

9. **100%** =

10. **90%** =

11. **47%** =

12. **800%** =

13. **15%** =

14. **22%** =

15. **13%** =

16. **205%** =

Total Problems 16 Problems Correct ____

Name_____   Skill: Changing Percentages to Fractions

Change the following percentages to fractions.

1. **20% =**   2. **31% =**   3. **28% =**   4. **10% =**

5. **5% =**   6. **18% =**   7. **22% =**   8. **88% =**

9. **77% =**   10. **12% =**   11. **30% =**   12. **20% =**

13. **9% =**   14. **11% =**   15. **6% =**   16. **188% =**

Total Problems __16__ Problems Correct ____

Name_____ Skill: Changing Percentages to Decimals

Change each percentage to a decimal.

1. **160% =**

2. **45% =**

3. **28% =**

4. **90% =**

5. **37% =**

6. **26% =**

7. **89% =**

8. **51% =**

9. **300% =**

10. **20% =**

11. **77% =**

12. **132% =**

13. **45% =**

14. **64% =**

15. **79% =**

16. **635% =**

Total Problems __16__ Problems Correct ____

Name_____ Skill: Changing Percentages to Decimals

Change each percentage to a decimal.

1. **90% =**   2. **21% =**   3. **46% =**   4. **79% =**

5. **9% =**   6. **75% =**   7. **18% =**   8. **44% =**

9. **33% =**   10. **19% =**   11. **25% =**   12. **80% =**

13. **2% =**   14. **29% =**   15. **1% =**   16. **456% =**

Total Problems __16__ Problems Correct ____

Name________________________

Skill: Fractions, Decimals, and Percentages Review

Complete the chart below.

	Fraction	Decimal	Percentage
1.			480%
2.		.75	
3.	$\frac{7}{20}$		
4.			20%
5.			28%
6.	$3\frac{3}{4}$		
7.	$2\frac{1}{5}$		
8.	$3\frac{7}{10}$		
9.		.9	

Total Problems _9_ Problems Correct ____

Name_____   Skill: Finding Percentages

Solve. Write your answers in simplest form.

1. **8% of 200 = _____**

2. **5% of 80 = _____**

3. **15% of 210 = _____**

4. **25% of 216 = _____**

5. **5% of 95 = _____**

6. **50% of 32 = _____**

7. **80% of 75 = _____**

8. **90% of 12 = _____**

9. **14% of 65 = _____**

10. **22% of 87 = _____**

11 **61% of 45 = _____**

12. **74% of 50 = _____**

13. **16% of 110 = _____**

14. **50% of 87 = _____**

Total Problems _14_ Problems Correct ____

Solve. Write your answers in simplest form.

1. **50% of 125 = _____**

2. **15% of 342 = _____**

3. **47% of 70 = _____**

4. **10% of 14 = _____**

5. **15% of 60 = _____**

6. **25% of 350 = _____**

7. **15% of 48 = _____**

8. **30% of 10 = _____**

9. **20% of 96 = _____**

10. **12% of 80 = _____**

11 **75% of 340 = _____**

12. **45% of 30 = _____**

13. **10% of 962 = _____**

14. **4% of 280 = _____**

Total Problems __14__ Problems Correct ____

Solve. Write your answers in simplest form.

1. **50% of 220 = _____**   2. **12% of 144 = _____**

3. **42% of 30 = _____**   4. **12% of 18 = _____**

5. **15% of 60 = _____**   6. **20% of 300 = _____**

7. **25% of 40 = _____**   8. **34% of 14 = _____**

9. **80% of 100 = _____**   10. **17% of 7 = _____**

11 **65% of 300 = _____**   12. **35% of 50 = _____**

13. **12% of 802 = _____**   14. **6% of 110 = _____**

Total Problems __14__ Problems Correct ____

Skill: Finding Percentages

Solve. Round each answer to the nearest tenth or hundredth.

1. **25 is _____% of 100**

2. **80 is _____% of 40**

3. **32 is _____% of 150**

4. **90 is _____% of 110**

5. **27 is _____% of 50**

6. **48 is _____% of 98**

7. **36 is _____% of 60**

8. **50 is _____% of 325**

9. **18 is _____% of 430**

10. **2 is _____% of 26**

11. **13 is _____% of 52**

12. **8 is _____% of 225**

13. **5 is _____% of 14**

14. **10 is _____% of 100**

Total Problems _14_ Problems Correct ____

Name_____   Skill: Finding Percentages

Solve. Round each answer to the nearest tenth or hundredth.

1. **63 is _____% of 70**

2. **21 is _____% of 70**

3. **168 is _____% of 110**

4. **24 is _____% of 60**

5. **90 is _____% of 72**

6. **18 is _____% of 30**

7. **903 is _____% of 420**

8. **225 is _____% of 150**

9. **18 is _____% of 430**

10. **2 is _____% of 26**

11. **8 is _____% of 20**

12. **5 is _____% of 4**

13. **20 is _____% of 8**

14. **9 is _____% of 120**

Total Problems 14 Problems Correct ____

Solve. Round each answer to the nearest tenth or hundredth.

1. **18 is 90% of _____**

2. **25 is 30% of _____**

3. **47 is 20% of _____**

4. **10 is 40% of _____**

5. **55 is 34% of _____**

6. **35 is 125% of _____**

7. **14 is 28% of _____**

8. **97 is 82% of _____**

9. **27 is 300% of _____**

10. **63 is 50% of _____**

11 **19 is 100% of _____**

12. **15 is 47% of _____**

13. **37 is 40% of _____**

14. **75 is 200% of _____**

Total Problems _14_ Problems Correct ____

Name_____   Skill: Finding Percentages

Solve. Round each answer to the nearest tenth or hundredth.

1. **30 is 45% of _____**   2. **22 is 80% of _____**

3. **40 is 20% of _____**   4. **42 is 50% of _____**

5. **6 is 40% of _____**   6. **10 is 90% of _____**

7. **12 is 30% of _____**   8. **95 is 80% of _____**

9. **48 is 4% of _____**   10. **4 is 48% of _____**

11. **6 is 3% of _____**   12. **16 is 28% of _____**

13. **87 is 10% of _____**   14. **9 is 50% of _____**

Total Problems _14_ Problems Correct ____

Solve. Round each answer to the nearest tenth or hundredth.

1. _____ is 90% of 140

2. _____ is 200% of 6

3. _____ is 40% of 120

4. _____ is 68% of 95

5. _____ is 70% of 90

6. _____ is 25% of 150

7. _____ is 45% of 130

8. _____ is 55% of 15

9. _____ is 75% of 138

10. _____ is 15% of 90

11 _____ is 12% of 118

12. _____ is 28% of 218

13. _____ is 19% of 290

14. _____ is 35% of 560

Total Problems __14__ Problems Correct ____

Name_____   Skill: Finding Percentages

Solve. Round each answer to the nearest tenth or hundredth.

1. _____ is 14% of 50   2. _____ is 21% of 85

3. _____ is 37% of 88   4. _____ is 32% of 75

5. _____ is 52% of 30   6. _____ is 55% of 93

7. _____ is 48% of 80   8. _____ is 23% of 54

9. _____ is 18% of 55   10. _____ is 74% of 39

11 _____ is 16% of 95   12. _____ is 45% of 60

13. _____ is 24% of 98   14. _____ is 35% of 70

Total Problems __14__ Problems Correct ____

Name_____   Skill: Calculating Interest

Calculate the amount of interest for the following. Round to the nearest cent. Use the formula, **Interest = Principal x rate x time**.

	Principal	Rate	Time	Interest
1.	$400.00	8%	1 year	
2.	$300.00	4%	1 year	
3.	$150.00	15%	2 years	
4.	$75.00	4%	4 years	
5.	$800.00	25%	3 years	
6.	$35.50	16%	3 years	
7.	$22.45	9%	2 years	
8.	$239.00	18%	1 year	
9.	$16.00	3%	5 years	
10.	$573.00	7%	7 years	

Total Problems 10   Problems Correct ____

Name_____   Skill: Calculating Interest

Calculate the amount of interest for the following. Round to the nearest cent. Use the formula, **Interest = Principal x rate x time**.

	Principal	Rate	Time	Interest
1.	$42.50	20%	4 years	
2.	$135.25	4.8%	8 years	
3.	$874.00	9%	2 years	
4.	$502.00	5.25%	3 years	
5.	$139.00	16.4%	7 years	
6.	$287.35	8.5%	1 year	
7.	$495.50	36%	2 years	
8.	$1,397.00	6.5%	5 years	
9.	$428.78	5.42%	3 years	
10.	$309.53	8.7%	4 years	

Total Problems 10   Problems Correct ____

74

Name_____   Skill: Naming Lines, Line Segments,
                                              and Rays

Name the following lines, line segments, or rays.

1. _____

2. _____

3. _____

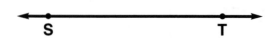

4. _____

5. _____

6. _____

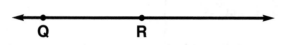

7. _____

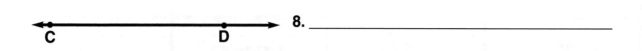

8. _____

Total Problems _8_ Problems Correct ____

75

Tell whether the following lines are parallel, intersecting, or perpendicular.

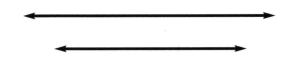

1. _____

2. _____

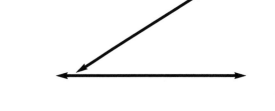

3. _____

4. _____

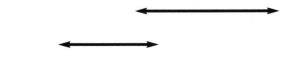

5. _____

6. _____

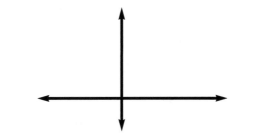

7. _____

8. _____

Total Problems 8 Problems Correct ____

Name each angle and write whether it is a right angle, an acute angle, or an obtuse angle.

1.

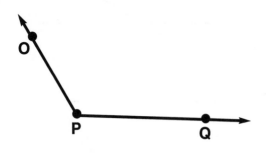

_____

2.

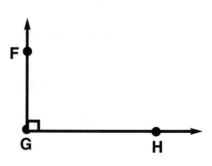

_____

3.

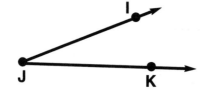

_____

4.

_____

5.

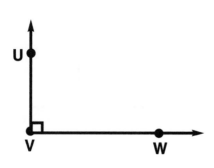

_____

6.

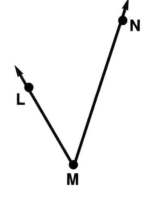

_____

Total Problems 6 Problems Correct ____

Name_____ Skill: Identifying Triangles

Write whether each triangle is a right triangle, an acute triangle,
or an obtuse triangle.

1.

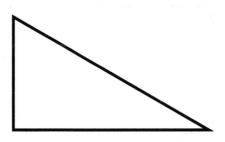

_____

2.

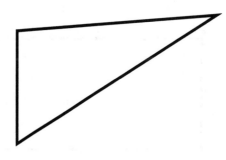

_____

3.

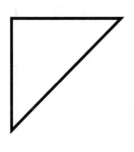

_____

4.

_____

5.

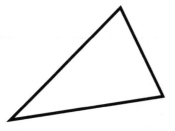

_____

6.

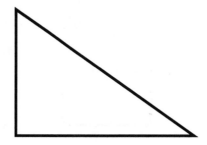

_____

Total Problems __6__ Problems Correct ____

Measure the sides of each rectangle in centimeters and inches. Write the most precise measurement of the longest or shortest side in centimeters or inches.

1.

_____

2.

_____

3.

_____

4.

_____

5.

_____

6.

_____

Total Problems 6   Problems Correct _____

Name_____   Skill: Measurement

Measure the sides of each square or rectangle in centimeters and inches. Write the most precise measurement of the longest or shortest side in centimeters or inches.

1.

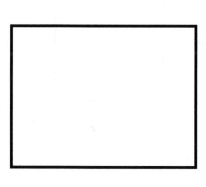

_____

2.

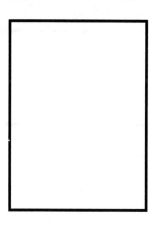

_____

3.

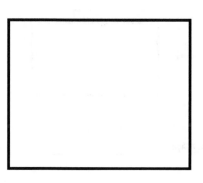

_____

4.

_____

5.

_____

6.

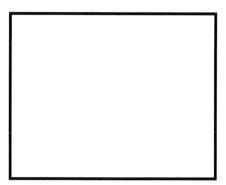

_____

Total Problems _6_ Problems Correct _____

Find the area of the following rectangles or squares. Use the formula,
Area = length x width.

1.

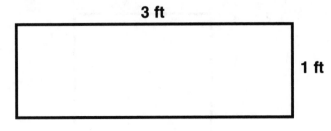

3 ft

1 ft

Area = _____

2.

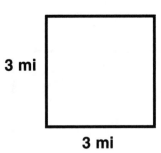

3 mi

3 mi

Area = _____

3.

7 cm

2 cm

Area = _____

4.

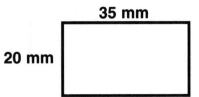

35 mm

20 mm

Area = _____

5.

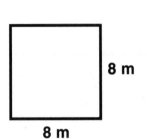

8 m

8 m

Area = _____

6.

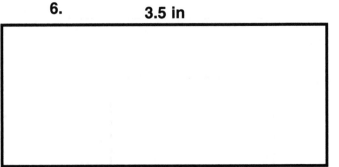

3.5 in

1.5 in

Area = _____

Total Problems _6_ Problems Correct ____

Name_____

Find the area of each rectangle and square.

1.

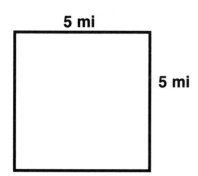

Area = _____

2.

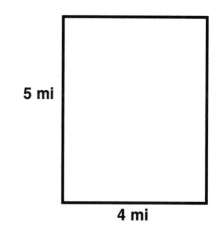

Area = _____

3.

21 m

6 m

Area = _____

4.

12 ft

1 ft

Area = _____

5.

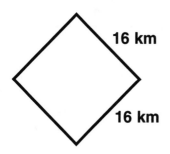

16 km

16 km

Area = _____

6.

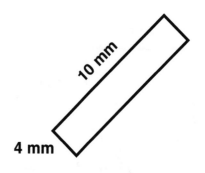

10 mm

4 mm

Area = _____

Total Problems _6_ Problems Correct ____

Name_____

Find the perimeter of the following figures.

1.

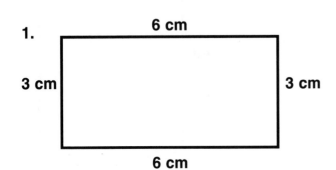

6 cm

3 cm   3 cm

6 cm

Perimeter = _____

2.

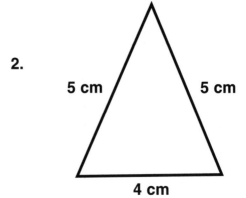

5 cm   5 cm

4 cm

Perimeter = _____

3.

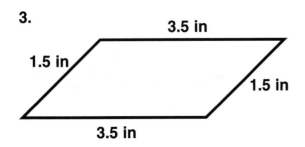

3.5 in

1.5 in

1.5 in

3.5 in

Perimeter = _____

4.

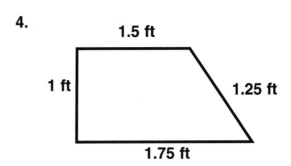

1.5 ft

1 ft   1.25 ft

1.75 ft

Perimeter = _____

5.

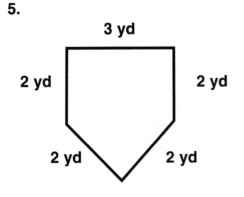

3 yd

2 yd   2 yd

2 yd   2 yd

Perimeter = _____

6.

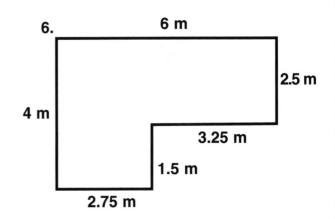

6 m

2.5 m

4 m

3.25 m

1.5 m

2.75 m

Perimeter = _____

Total Problems _6_ Problems Correct ____

Name_____   Skill: Finding Perimeter

Find the perimeter of each shape.

1.

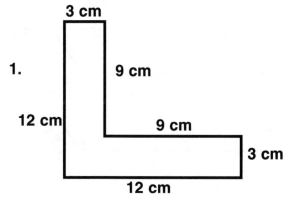

Perimeter = _____

2.

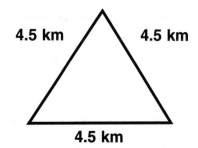

Perimeter = _____

3.

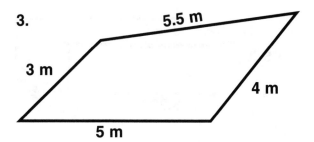

Perimeter = _____

4.

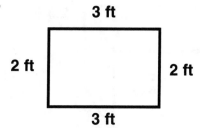

Perimeter = _____

5.

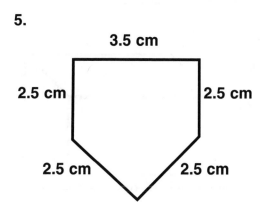

Perimeter = _____

6.

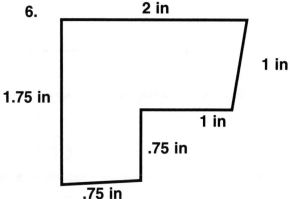

Perimeter = _____

Total Problems __6__ Problems Correct ____

84

Name_____

Find the volume of the following rectangular solids. Use the formula,
Volume = length x width x height.

1.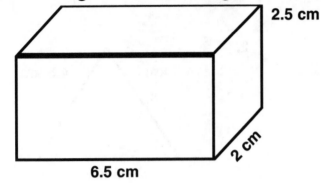

2.75 cm

2 cm

6.5 cm

Volume = _____

2.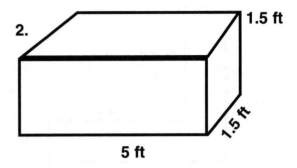

1.5 ft

1.5 ft

5 ft

Volume = _____

3.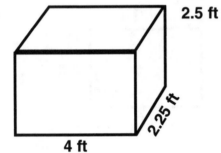

2.5 ft

2.25 ft

4 ft

Volume = _____

4.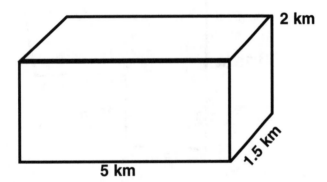

1.5 ft

5.25 ft

2.25 ft

Volume = _____

5.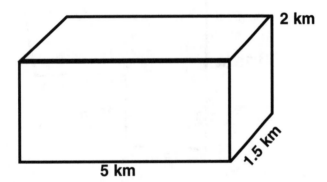

2 km

1.5 km

5 km

Volume = _____

6.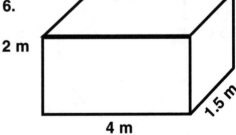

2 m

1.5 m

4 m

Volume = _____

Total Problems _6_ Problems Correct ____

Name_____   Skill: Finding the Area of Circles

Use the appropriate formula to find the area of each circle:
Area = 3.14 x radius x radius   OR   Area = 3.14 x (diameter ÷ 2)²

1.

Area = _____

2.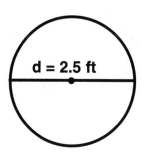

Area = _____

3.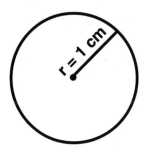

Area = _____

4.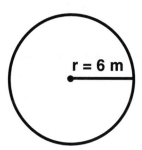

Area = _____

5.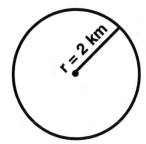

Area = _____

6.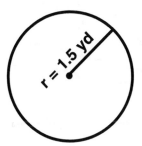

Area = _____

Total Problems __6__   Problems Correct _____

Name_____   Skill: Finding the Area of Triangles

Find the area of the following triangles. Use the formula, **Area = $\frac{1}{2}$x (base x height)**.

1.

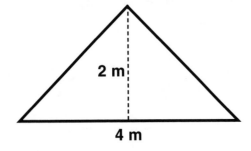

2 m

4 m

2.

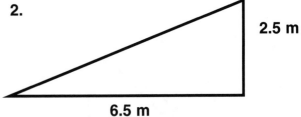

2.5 m

6.5 m

Area = _____

Area = _____

3.

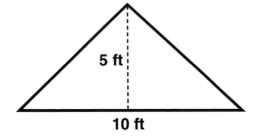

5 ft

10 ft

4.

100 km

275 km

Area = _____

Area = _____

5.

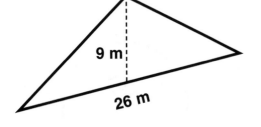

9 m

26 m

6.

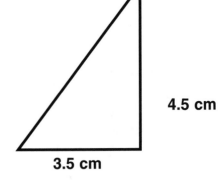

4.5 cm

3.5 cm

Area = _____

Area = _____

Total Problems 6   Problems Correct ____

Use the graph to answer the following questions.

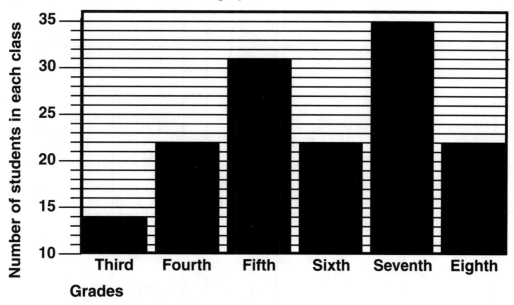

1. How many students are in the sixth grade? _____

2. Which class has the most students? _____

3. Which class has the least students? _____

4. What is the mean number of students in class? _____

5. What number of students represents the mode in this set of data? _____

6. What is the range of students in class?_____

Use the graph to answer the following questions.

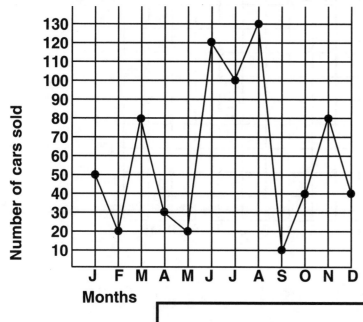

1. In which months were at least 120 cars sold? _____

2. Which month had the highest number of sales? _____

3. What is the mean number of cars sold per month? _____

4. What is the range in the number of cars sold? _____

5. What is the median number of cars sold? _____

Total Problems __11__ Problems Correct ____

Identify the points.

1. A (___,___)
2. B (___,___)
3. C (___,___)
4. D (___,___)
5. E (___,___)
6. F (___,___)
7. G (___,___)
8. H (___,___)
9. I (___,___)
10. J (___,___)

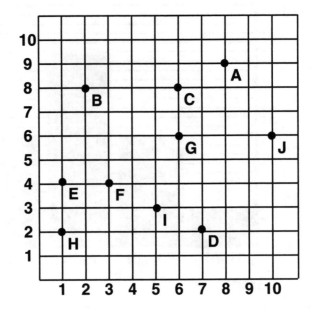

Identify the points.

1. A (___,___)
2. B (___,___)
3. C (___,___)
4. D (___,___)
5. E (___,___)
6. F (___,___)
7. G (___,___)
8. H (___,___)
9. I (___,___)
10. J (___,___)

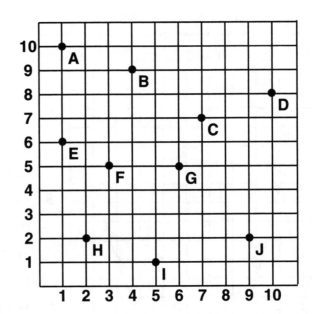

Total Problems _20_ Problems Correct ____

Name_____

Use the following information to make a line graph. First, title the graph. Next, name the X axis *Months* and the Y axis *Number of Students*, and label the graph. Finally, plot the data.

Number of students on the honor roll per month.

January	13
February	20
March	17
April	25
May	12
September	15
October	14
November	21
December	25

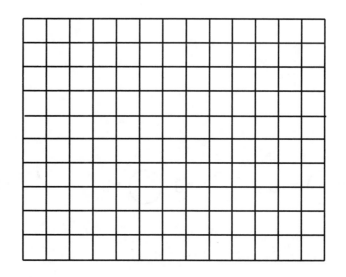

Use the following information to make a line graph. First, title the graph. Next, name the X axis *Week Number* and the Y axis *Houses Sold,* and label the graph. Finally, plot the data.

Week No.	Houses Sold
1	3
2	8
3	7
4	4
5	5
6	6
7	10
8	5
9	4
10	6

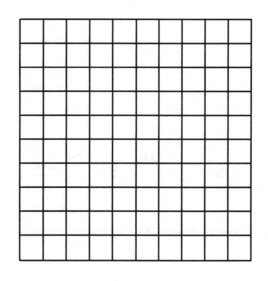

Total Problems 2   Problems Correct ____

Fill in the circle with **<, >**, or **=** to make each statement true.

1. 2 ◯ -2

2. -5 ◯ -7

3. -1 ◯ 1

4. 4 ◯ -3

5. -6 ◯ -10

6. -6 ◯ -9

7. -1 ◯ 2

8. -6 ◯ 3

9. -3 ◯ 1

10. -2 ◯ 0

11. 5 ◯ 0

12. -6 ◯ 5

13. -3 ◯ -9

14. 9 ◯ -2

15. 4 ◯ -2

16. -3 ◯ -5

Total Problems __16__ Problems Correct ____

Rewrite each set of integers in order from the least to the greatest.

1.   -2, -5, -4, 6, -10 _____

2.   7, -5, -3, 3, -8 _____

3.   2, -1, 4, -6, 10 _____

4.   -10, 5, 4, -4, -8 _____

5.   5, -4, 3, 7, -8 _____

6.   4, -4, -1, 3, -2 _____

7.   2, 5, -12, 10, -5 _____

8.   8, 2, -7, 6, 7 _____

9.   -9, -12, 4, 8, 1 _____

10.   -6, 5, -4, 16, -1 _____

Total Problems 10 Problems Correct ____

Name_____   Skill: Adding and Subtracting Integers

Add or subtract.

1. $3 + {}^-5 =$

2. ${}^-4 + {}^-2 =$

3. ${}^-6 + 4 =$

4. $10 + {}^-10 =$

5. ${}^-6 + 3 =$

6. ${}^-4 + {}^-8 =$

7. ${}^-1 + {}^-8 =$

8. $5 + 6 =$

9. $9 + {}^-8 =$

10. $4 - {}^-3 =$

11. ${}^-4 - {}^-5 =$

12. ${}^-9 - 5 =$

13. $10 - {}^-11 =$

14. ${}^-8 - 8 =$

15. ${}^-2 - {}^-4 =$

16. ${}^-7 - {}^-8 =$

17. $5 - 6 =$

18. $6 - {}^-8 =$

Total Problems 18   Problems Correct ____

Skill: Finding Exponents

Solve using a calculator.

1. $10^9 =$

2. $8^6 =$

3. $7^9 =$

4. $4^6 =$

5. $9^8 =$

6. $10^7 =$

7. $6^5 =$

8. $5^7 =$

9. $3^8 =$

10. $2^{10} =$

11. $8^5 =$

12. $9^3 =$

13. $3^9 =$

14. $1^{10} =$

15. $7^4 =$

16. $5^3 =$

Total Problems __16__ Problems Correct ____

Name_____   Skill: Finding Exponents

Solve without using a calculator.

1. $1^5 =$ 2. $6^2 =$ 3. $10^3 =$ 4. $3^2 =$

5. $4^4 =$ 6. $7^2 =$ 7. $2^4 =$ 8. $5^5 =$

9. $8^2 =$ 10. $9^4 =$ 11. $10^8 =$ 12. $3^5 =$

13. $7^3 =$ 14. $2^9 =$ 15. $6^4 =$ 16. $8^3 =$

Total Problems 16 Problems Correct ____

95

Answer Key

Name_____   Skill: Adding Two, Three, Four, and Five Digit Numbers

Add.

1.	2.	3.	4.	5.
42 + 12 54	55 + 64 119	83 + 12 95	48 + 62 110	55 + 90 145
6. 234 + 195 429	7. 558 + 317 875	8. 633 + 349 982	9. 458 + 852 1,310	10. 245 + 456 701
11. 5,214 + 827 6,041	12. 1,654 + 203 1,857	13. 3,122 + 408 3,530	14. 3,961 + 990 4,951	15. 4,311 + 595 4,906
16. 1,700 + 2,126 3,826	17. 8,909 + 6,667 15,576	18. 4,621 + 5,841 10,462	19. 3,031 + 4,275 7,306	20. 6,762 + 1,136 7,898
21. 81,037 + 94,539 175,576	22. 32,441 + 10,254 42,695	23. 54,622 + 62,854 117,476	24. 40,148 + 27,834 67,982	

Total Problems _24_ Problems Correct ____

© Carson-Dellosa CD-3749   1

Name_____   Skill: Adding Two, Three, Four, and Five Digit Numbers

Add.

1.	2.	3.	4.	5.
66 + 21 87	38 + 45 83	43 + 28 71	74 + 20 94	95 + 89 184
6. 185 + 122 307	7. 399 + 421 820	8. 159 + 179 338	9. 128 + 397 525	10. 742 + 325 1,067
11. 1,214 + 854 2,068	12. 4,781 + 125 4,906	13. 3,214 + 285 3,499	14. 2,325 + 456 2,781	15. 7,951 + 351 8,302
16. 1,780 + 4,522 6,302	17. 7,919 + 6,328 14,247	18. 2,852 + 3,122 5,974	19. 3,188 + 4,357 7,545	20. 6,851 + 1,111 7,962
21. 81,037 + 23,539 104,576	22. 62,264 + 13,142 75,406	23. 75,421 + 72,840 148,261	24. 49,122 + 87,834 136,956	

Total Problems _24_ Problems Correct ____

© Carson-Dellosa CD-3749   2

Name_____   Skill: Adding Two, Three, Four, and Five Digit Numbers

Add.

1.	2.	3.	4.	5.
584 845 + 217 1,646	560 884 + 551 1,995	385 256 + 382 1,023	882 456 + 127 1,465	541 241 + 369 1,151
6. 2,456 8,445 + 2,778 13,679	7. 3,570 2,869 + 2,210 8,649	8. 4,687 4,258 + 6,621 15,566	9. 5,285 1,124 + 5,038 11,447	10. 3,221 4,654 + 6,213 14,088
11. 40,554 5,654 + 3,122 49,330	12. 69,721 21,065 + 2,985 93,771	13. 4,349 88 + 524 4,961	14. 21,254 51,342 + 852 73,448	15. 68,695 3,072 + 210 71,977
16. 47,107 52,001 42,932 + 207 142,247	17. 5,045 622 18 + 5 5,690	18. 5,840 636 59 + 2,129 8,664	19. 2,215 782 560 + 49 3,606	20. 8,841 654 9,388 + 78 18,961

Total Problems _20_ Problems Correct ____

© Carson-Dellosa CD-3749   3

Name_____   Skill: Subtracting Two and Three Digit Numbers

Subtract.

1.	2.	3.	4.	5.
451 − 35 416	588 − 22 566	358 − 62 296	535 − 23 512	525 − 78 447
6. 147 − 65 82	7. 325 − 58 267	8. 352 − 21 331	9. 817 − 24 793	10. 622 − 45 577
11. 467 − 457 10	12. 865 − 255 610	13. 921 − 650 271	14. 885 − 214 671	15. 841 − 562 279
16. 951 − 123 828	17. 725 − 582 143	18. 540 − 185 355	19. 806 − 652 154	20. 885 − 504 381
21. 721 − 129 592	22. 784 − 694 90	23. 456 − 283 173	24. 345 − 116 229	25. 668 − 422 246

Total Problems _25_ Problems Correct ____

© Carson-Dellosa CD-3749   4

Answer Key

Name_____ Skill: Subtracting Two, Three, Four, Five,
and Six Digit Numbers

Subtract.

1. 6,567 − 52 **6,515**	2. 6,232 − 25 **6,207**	3. 8,421 − 88 **8,333**	4. 9,219 − 85 **9,134**	5. 1,359 − 28 **1,331**
6. 5,487 − 225 **5,262**	7. 5,512 − 808 **4,704**	8. 7,247 − 448 **6,799**	9. 8,824 − 488 **8,336**	10. 5,427 − 131 **5,296**
11. 45,107 − 3,458 **41,649**	12. 51,257 − 4,071 **47,186**	13. 46,687 − 5,674 **41,013**	14. 52,399 − 1,008 **51,391**	15. 56,571 − 6,221 **50,350**
16. 86,961 − 71,831 **15,130**	17. 87,810 − 52,516 **35,294**	18. 35,300 − 28,704 **6,596**	19. 96,127 − 73,279 **22,848**	
20. 472,175 − 68,189 **403,986**	21. 566,502 − 10,498 **556,004**	22. 227,645 − 53,217 **174,428**	23. 517,523 − 46,211 **471,312**	

Total Problems __23__ Problems Correct ____

5

Name_____ Skill: Multiplying Two and Three
Digit Numbers

Multiply.

1. 52 x 48 **2,496**	2. 75 x 52 **3,900**	3. 43 x 71 **3,053**	4. 62 x 82 **5,084**	5. 35 x 17 **595**
6. 21 x 11 **231**	7. 98 x 93 **9,114**	8. 31 x 41 **1,271**	9. 77 x 65 **5,005**	10. 45 x 50 **2,250**
11. 84 x 21 **1,764**	12. 22 x 17 **374**	13. 47 x 38 **1,786**	14. 48 x 52 **2,496**	15. 98 x 40 **3,920**
16. 685 x 21 **14,385**	17. 322 x 23 **7,406**	18. 724 x 43 **31,132**	19. 518 x 59 **30,562**	20. 42 x 57 **2,394**

Total Problems __20__ Problems Correct ____

6

Name_____ Skill: Multiplying Two and Three
Digit Numbers

Multiply.

1. 23 x 45 **1,035**	2. 85 x 61 **5,185**	3. 22 x 12 **264**	4. 87 x 56 **4872**	5. 34 x 22 **748**
6. 41 x 35 **1,435**	7. 62 x 51 **3,162**	8. 39 x 49 **1,911**	9. 88 x 25 **2,200**	10. 33 x 12 **396**
11. 21 x 31 **651**	12. 48 x 62 **2,976**	13. 38 x 22 **836**	14. 39 x 54 **2,106**	15. 90 x 12 **1,080**
16. 225 x 17 **3,825**	17. 854 x 56 **47,824**	18. 885 x 95 **84,075**	19. 369 x 84 **30,996**	20. 215 x 66 **14,190**

Total Problems __20__ Problems Correct ____

7

Name_____ Skill: Multiplying Two, Three, and Four
Digit Numbers

Multiply.

1. 885 x 62 **54,870**	2. 558 x 31 **17,298**	3. 668 x 51 **34,068**	4. 830 x 95 **78,850**	5. 741 x 51 **37,791**
6. 611 x 231 **141,141**	7. 729 x 106 **77,274**	8. 147 x 535 **78,645**	9. 844 x 462 **389,928**	10. 512 x 787 **402,944**
11. 818 x 500 **409,000**	12. 271 x 235 **63,685**	13. 682 x 623 **424,886**	14. 431 x 638 **274,978**	15. 335 x 213 **71,355**
16. 8,242 x 682 **5,621,044**	17. 3,851 x 492 **1,894,692**	18. 4,341 x 863 **3,746,283**	19. 7,433 x 682 **5,069,306**	20. 892 x 214 **190,888**

Total Problems __20__ Problems Correct ____

8

Answer Key

Name_____   Skill: Dividing by One Digit Numbers

Divide.

1. $8\overline{)64}$ = 8
2. $9\overline{)81}$ = 9
3. $7\overline{)42}$ = 6
4. $8\overline{)56}$ = 7
5. $6\overline{)24}$ = 4

6. $5\overline{)25}$ = 5
7. $8\overline{)24}$ = 3
8. $6\overline{)54}$ = 9
9. $8\overline{)16}$ = 2
10. $9\overline{)90}$ = 10

11. $6\overline{)30}$ = 5
12. $7\overline{)77}$ = 11
13. $6\overline{)36}$ = 6
14. $5\overline{)35}$ = 7
15. $9\overline{)63}$ = 7

16. $5\overline{)40}$ = 8
17. $8\overline{)32}$ = 4
18. $3\overline{)12}$ = 4
19. $7\overline{)14}$ = 2
20. $6\overline{)60}$ = 10

21. $4\overline{)20}$ = 5
22. $9\overline{)27}$ = 3
23. $5\overline{)30}$ = 6
24. $9\overline{)36}$ = 4
25. $9\overline{)63}$ = 7

Total Problems _25_ Problems Correct ____

© Carson-Dellosa CD-3749
9

Name_____   Skill: Dividing by Two Digit Numbers

Divide.

1. $22\overline{)308}$ = 14
2. $11\overline{)286}$ = 26
3. $16\overline{)832}$ = 52
4. $41\overline{)574}$ = 14

5. $17\overline{)306}$ = 18
6. $33\overline{)957}$ = 29
7. $53\overline{)901}$ = 17
8. $62\overline{)744}$ = 12

9. $24\overline{)1,200}$ = 50
10. $38\overline{)1,064}$ = 28
11. $45\overline{)1,485}$ = 33
12. $57\overline{)3,591}$ = 63

13. $86\overline{)4,730}$ = 55
14. $74\overline{)3,848}$ = 52
15. $91\overline{)5,096}$ = 56
16. $18\overline{)1,296}$ = 72

17. $73\overline{)4,453}$ = 61
18. $29\overline{)1,798}$ = 62
19. $82\overline{)1,968}$ = 24
20. $95\overline{)3,990}$ = 42

Total Problems _20_ Problems Correct ____

© Carson-Dellosa CD-3749
10

Name_____   Skill: Changing Fractions to Simplest Form

Change each fraction or mixed number to simplest form.

1. $\frac{6}{8} = \frac{3}{4}$
2. $\frac{2}{4} = \frac{1}{2}$
3. $\frac{15}{18} = \frac{5}{6}$
4. $\frac{16}{24} = \frac{2}{3}$
5. $\frac{10}{40} = \frac{1}{4}$

6. $\frac{6}{15} = \frac{2}{5}$
7. $\frac{2}{10} = \frac{1}{5}$
8. $\frac{20}{40} = \frac{1}{2}$
9. $\frac{16}{32} = \frac{1}{2}$
10. $\frac{56}{64} = \frac{7}{8}$

11. $\frac{27}{81} = \frac{1}{3}$
12. $\frac{12}{24} = \frac{1}{2}$
13. $\frac{10}{15} = \frac{2}{3}$
14. $\frac{14}{21} = \frac{2}{3}$
15. $\frac{25}{30} = \frac{5}{6}$

16. $2\frac{24}{30} = 2\frac{4}{5}$
17. $3\frac{12}{18} = 3\frac{2}{3}$
18. $1\frac{18}{20} = 1\frac{9}{10}$
19. $4\frac{3}{24} = 4\frac{1}{8}$

20. $4\frac{4}{8} = 4\frac{1}{2}$
21. $5\frac{10}{15} = 5\frac{2}{3}$
22. $3\frac{6}{9} = 3\frac{2}{3}$
23. $2\frac{8}{32} = 2\frac{1}{4}$

Total Problems _23_ Problems Correct ____

© Carson-Dellosa CD-3749
11

Name_____   Skill: Changing Fractions to Simplest Form

Change each fraction or mixed number to simplest form.

1. $\frac{4}{8} = \frac{1}{2}$
2. $\frac{2}{8} = \frac{1}{4}$
3. $\frac{15}{21} = \frac{5}{7}$
4. $\frac{16}{20} = \frac{4}{5}$
5. $\frac{10}{60} = \frac{1}{6}$

6. $\frac{4}{16} = \frac{1}{4}$
7. $\frac{3}{12} = \frac{1}{4}$
8. $\frac{30}{40} = \frac{3}{4}$
9. $\frac{12}{32} = \frac{3}{8}$
10. $\frac{49}{63} = \frac{7}{9}$

11. $\frac{28}{70} = \frac{2}{5}$
12. $\frac{13}{39} = \frac{1}{3}$
13. $\frac{12}{15} = \frac{4}{5}$
14. $\frac{18}{36} = \frac{1}{2}$
15. $\frac{9}{9} = 1$

16. $1\frac{36}{48} = 1\frac{3}{4}$
17. $3\frac{15}{30} = 3\frac{1}{2}$
18. $2\frac{18}{20} = 2\frac{9}{10}$
19. $6\frac{3}{12} = 6\frac{1}{4}$

20. $5\frac{3}{9} = 5\frac{1}{3}$
21. $4\frac{12}{15} = 4\frac{4}{5}$
22. $5\frac{7}{7} = 6$
23. $4\frac{9}{36} = 4\frac{1}{4}$

Total Problems _23_ Problems Correct ____

© Carson-Dellosa CD-3749
12

Answer Key

Name_____ Skill: Changing Mixed Numbers to Fractions

Change each mixed number to a fraction.

1. $2\frac{5}{8} = \frac{21}{8}$
2. $4\frac{1}{2} = \frac{9}{2}$
3. $6\frac{3}{4} = \frac{27}{4}$

4. $3\frac{6}{7} = \frac{27}{7}$
5. $8\frac{7}{8} = \frac{71}{8}$
6. $2\frac{1}{9} = \frac{19}{9}$

7. $8\frac{5}{11} = \frac{93}{11}$
8. $3\frac{3}{10} = \frac{33}{10}$
9. $4\frac{5}{12} = \frac{53}{12}$

10. $8\frac{2}{3} = \frac{26}{3}$
11. $2\frac{3}{5} = \frac{13}{5}$
12. $5\frac{5}{7} = \frac{40}{7}$

Total Problems _12_ Problems Correct ____

© Carson-Dellosa CD- 3749

13

Name_____ Skill: Changing Mixed Numbers to Fractions

Change each mixed number to a fraction.

1. $3\frac{5}{9} = \frac{32}{9}$
2. $3\frac{1}{3} = \frac{10}{3}$
3. $5\frac{2}{4} = \frac{22}{4}$

4. $5\frac{6}{8} = \frac{46}{8}$
5. $7\frac{3}{5} = \frac{38}{5}$
6. $4\frac{1}{6} = \frac{25}{6}$

7. $7\frac{4}{10} = \frac{74}{10}$
8. $2\frac{7}{11} = \frac{29}{11}$
9. $1\frac{6}{12} = \frac{18}{12}$

10. $5\frac{2}{3} = \frac{17}{3}$
11. $7\frac{3}{5} = \frac{38}{5}$
12. $3\frac{5}{7} = \frac{26}{7}$

Total Problems _12_ Problems Correct ____

© Carson-Dellosa CD- 3749

14

Name_____ Skill: Changing Fractions to Mixed Numbers

Change each fraction to a mixed number.

1. $\frac{13}{7} = 1\frac{6}{7}$
2. $\frac{10}{6} = 1\frac{2}{3}$

3. $\frac{32}{7} = 4\frac{4}{7}$
4. $\frac{21}{16} = 1\frac{5}{16}$

5. $\frac{37}{14} = 2\frac{9}{14}$
6. $\frac{55}{19} = 2\frac{17}{19}$

7. $\frac{12}{5} = 2\frac{2}{5}$
8. $\frac{14}{13} = 1\frac{1}{13}$

9. $\frac{50}{21} = 2\frac{8}{21}$
10. $\frac{43}{20} = 2\frac{3}{20}$

Total Problems _10_ Problems Correct ____

© Carson-Dellosa CD- 3749

15

Name_____ Skill: Changing Fractions to Mixed Numbers

Change each fraction to a mixed number.

1. $\frac{13}{5} = 2\frac{3}{5}$
2. $\frac{12}{5} = 2\frac{2}{5}$

3. $\frac{32}{7} = 4\frac{4}{7}$
4. $\frac{48}{17} = 2\frac{14}{17}$

5. $\frac{36}{11} = 3\frac{3}{11}$
6. $\frac{77}{20} = 3\frac{17}{20}$

7. $\frac{13}{4} = 3\frac{1}{4}$
8. $\frac{15}{12} = 1\frac{1}{4}$

9. $\frac{30}{21} = 1\frac{3}{7}$
10. $\frac{53}{22} = 2\frac{9}{22}$

Total Problems _10_ Problems Correct ____

© Carson-Dellosa CD- 3749

16

© Carson-Dellosa CD-3749

99

Answer Key

Name_____ Skill: Finding the Least Common Denominator

Find the least common denominator for each pair of fractions.

1. $\frac{1}{6}, \frac{2}{5}$ __30__

2. $\frac{1}{6}, \frac{3}{5}$ __30__

3. $\frac{2}{4}, \frac{1}{7}$ __28__

4. $\frac{1}{9}, \frac{2}{2}$ __18__

5. $\frac{3}{5}, \frac{3}{8}$ __40__

6. $\frac{2}{5}, \frac{1}{2}$ __10__

7. $\frac{1}{2}, \frac{3}{5}$ __10__

8. $\frac{5}{8}, \frac{3}{9}$ __72__

9. $\frac{3}{7}, \frac{1}{2}$ __14__

10. $\frac{7}{5}, \frac{2}{6}$ __30__

11. $\frac{3}{7}, \frac{1}{9}$ __63__

12. $\frac{1}{5}, \frac{1}{3}$ __15__

Total Problems __12__ Problems Correct ____

17

Name_____ Skill: Adding Fractions with the Same Denominators

Add. Write answers in simplest form.

1. $\frac{1}{4} + \frac{2}{4} = \frac{3}{4}$

2. $\frac{1}{5} + \frac{2}{5} = \frac{3}{5}$

3. $\frac{1}{6} + \frac{3}{6} = \frac{2}{3}$

4. $\frac{1}{9} + \frac{2}{9} = \frac{1}{3}$

5. $\frac{3}{8} + \frac{7}{8} = 1\frac{1}{4}$

6. $\frac{7}{11} + \frac{1}{11} = \frac{8}{11}$

7. $\frac{3}{6} + \frac{2}{6} = \frac{5}{6}$

8. $\frac{5}{9} + \frac{8}{9} = 1\frac{4}{9}$

9. $\frac{1}{2} + \frac{1}{2} = 1$

10. $\frac{2}{7} + \frac{4}{7} = \frac{6}{7}$

11. $\frac{7}{12} + \frac{2}{12} = \frac{3}{4}$

12. $\frac{2}{5} + \frac{5}{5} = 1\frac{2}{5}$

13. $\frac{5}{15} + \frac{2}{15} = \frac{7}{15}$

14. $\frac{9}{13} + \frac{8}{13} = 1\frac{4}{13}$

15. $\frac{9}{17} + \frac{8}{17} = 1$

Total Problems __15__ Problems Correct ____

18

Name_____ Skill: Adding Fractions with the Same Denominators

Add. Write answers in simplest form.

1. $\frac{1}{7}$
$+ \frac{2}{7}$
$\frac{3}{7}$

2. $\frac{1}{3}$
$+ \frac{2}{3}$
1

3. $\frac{4}{12}$
$+ \frac{5}{12}$
$\frac{3}{4}$

4. $\frac{6}{10}$
$+ \frac{7}{10}$
$1\frac{3}{10}$

5. $\frac{4}{6}$
$+ \frac{1}{6}$
$\frac{5}{6}$

6. $\frac{2}{7}$
$+ \frac{1}{7}$
$\frac{3}{7}$

7. $\frac{3}{15}$
$+ \frac{3}{15}$
$\frac{2}{5}$

8. $\frac{8}{11}$
$+ \frac{6}{11}$
$1\frac{3}{11}$

9. $\frac{5}{8}$
$+ \frac{1}{8}$
$\frac{3}{4}$

10. $\frac{1}{3}$
$+ \frac{2}{3}$
1

11. $\frac{2}{15}$
$+ \frac{4}{15}$
$\frac{2}{5}$

12. $\frac{4}{10}$
$+ \frac{2}{10}$
$\frac{3}{5}$

13. $\frac{4}{9}$
$+ \frac{2}{9}$
$\frac{2}{3}$

14. $\frac{10}{17}$
$+ \frac{11}{17}$
$1\frac{4}{17}$

15. $\frac{5}{18}$
$+ \frac{3}{18}$
$\frac{4}{9}$

16. $\frac{1}{2}$
$+ \frac{1}{2}$
1

Total Problems __16__ Problems Correct ____

19

Name_____ Skill: Adding Fractions With Different Denominators

Add. Write answers in simplest form.

1. $\frac{1}{2} + \frac{2}{5} = \frac{9}{10}$

2. $\frac{2}{3} + \frac{3}{5} = 1\frac{4}{15}$

3. $\frac{1}{4} + \frac{3}{8} = \frac{5}{8}$

4. $\frac{1}{6} + \frac{3}{4} = \frac{11}{12}$

5. $\frac{3}{7} + \frac{1}{3} = \frac{16}{21}$

6. $\frac{1}{10} + \frac{2}{20} = \frac{1}{5}$

7. $\frac{1}{8} + \frac{3}{4} = \frac{7}{8}$

8. $\frac{1}{9} + \frac{2}{7} = \frac{25}{63}$

9. $\frac{2}{5} + \frac{1}{3} = \frac{11}{15}$

10. $\frac{2}{3} + \frac{3}{4} = 1\frac{5}{12}$

11. $\frac{7}{10} + \frac{3}{12} = \frac{19}{20}$

12. $\frac{2}{5} + \frac{5}{6} = 1\frac{7}{30}$

13. $\frac{5}{12} + \frac{2}{10} = \frac{37}{60}$

14. $\frac{1}{6} + \frac{3}{5} = \frac{23}{30}$

15. $\frac{1}{4} + \frac{2}{7} = \frac{15}{28}$

Total Problems __15__ Problems Correct ____

20

100

Answer Key

Worksheet 21

Add. Write answers in simplest form.

1. $\dfrac{1}{4} + \dfrac{3}{5} = \dfrac{17}{20}$
2. $\dfrac{4}{5} + \dfrac{7}{8} = 1\dfrac{27}{40}$
3. $\dfrac{3}{6} + \dfrac{3}{4} = 1\dfrac{1}{4}$
4. $\dfrac{1}{3} + \dfrac{5}{7} = 1\dfrac{1}{21}$

5. $\dfrac{1}{2} + \dfrac{1}{5} = \dfrac{7}{10}$
6. $\dfrac{2}{3} + \dfrac{5}{6} = 1\dfrac{1}{2}$
7. $\dfrac{1}{4} + \dfrac{2}{3} = \dfrac{11}{12}$
8. $\dfrac{1}{3} + \dfrac{7}{8} = 1\dfrac{5}{24}$

9. $\dfrac{4}{5} + \dfrac{2}{3} = 1\dfrac{7}{15}$
10. $\dfrac{3}{4} + \dfrac{1}{3} = 1\dfrac{1}{12}$
11. $\dfrac{5}{8} + \dfrac{2}{3} = 1\dfrac{7}{24}$
12. $\dfrac{2}{3} + \dfrac{2}{10} = \dfrac{13}{15}$

13. $\dfrac{2}{3} + \dfrac{2}{5} = 1\dfrac{1}{15}$
14. $\dfrac{1}{6} + \dfrac{2}{5} = \dfrac{17}{30}$
15. $\dfrac{2}{5} + \dfrac{1}{3} = \dfrac{11}{15}$
16. $\dfrac{2}{7} + \dfrac{2}{3} = \dfrac{20}{21}$

Total Problems _16_ Problems Correct ____

© Carson-Dellosa CI 3749   21

Worksheet 22

Add. Write answers in simplest form.

1. $4\dfrac{1}{8} + 5\dfrac{3}{4} = 9\dfrac{7}{8}$
2. $6\dfrac{1}{2} + 6\dfrac{2}{5} = 12\dfrac{9}{10}$
3. $3\dfrac{1}{9} + 2\dfrac{1}{3} = 5\dfrac{4}{9}$

4. $4\dfrac{7}{8} + 6\dfrac{1}{4} = 11\dfrac{1}{8}$
5. $8\dfrac{1}{3} + 2\dfrac{3}{7} = 10\dfrac{16}{21}$
6. $5\dfrac{2}{3} + 7\dfrac{3}{7} = 13\dfrac{2}{21}$

7. $4\dfrac{3}{4} + 1\dfrac{2}{3} = 6\dfrac{5}{12}$
8. $5\dfrac{1}{8} + 6\dfrac{2}{5} = 11\dfrac{21}{40}$
9. $2\dfrac{5}{6} + 3\dfrac{1}{3} = 6\dfrac{1}{6}$

10. $4\dfrac{1}{8} + 5\dfrac{1}{5} = 9\dfrac{13}{40}$
11. $1\dfrac{9}{10} + 3\dfrac{1}{4} = 5\dfrac{3}{20}$
12. $5\dfrac{1}{2} + 6\dfrac{2}{7} = 11\dfrac{11}{14}$

13. $8\dfrac{3}{4} + 7\dfrac{3}{16} = 15\dfrac{15}{16}$
14. $2\dfrac{3}{4} + 3\dfrac{5}{6} = 6\dfrac{7}{12}$
15. $1\dfrac{3}{8} + 1\dfrac{1}{4} = 2\dfrac{5}{8}$

Total Problems _15_ Problems Correct ____

© Carson-Dellosa CD- 3749   22

Worksheet 23

Add. Write answers in simplest form.

1. $5\dfrac{1}{6} + 2\dfrac{3}{4} = 7\dfrac{11}{12}$
2. $3\dfrac{1}{3} + 4\dfrac{2}{5} = 7\dfrac{11}{15}$
3. $1\dfrac{1}{7} + 8\dfrac{1}{5} = 9\dfrac{12}{35}$

4. $4\dfrac{7}{8} + 6\dfrac{1}{3} = 11\dfrac{5}{24}$
5. $8\dfrac{1}{2} + 2\dfrac{3}{7} = 10\dfrac{13}{14}$
6. $5\dfrac{5}{8} + 7\dfrac{3}{7} = 12\dfrac{19}{28}$

7. $2\dfrac{3}{4} + 1\dfrac{2}{3} = 4\dfrac{5}{12}$
8. $7\dfrac{1}{8} + 5\dfrac{2}{5} = 12\dfrac{21}{40}$
9. $1\dfrac{5}{6} + 3\dfrac{1}{3} = 5\dfrac{1}{6}$

10. $3\dfrac{1}{8} + 5\dfrac{1}{6} = 8\dfrac{7}{24}$
11. $4\dfrac{9}{10} + 3\dfrac{1}{5} = 8\dfrac{1}{10}$
12. $5\dfrac{1}{4} + 6\dfrac{2}{7} = 11\dfrac{15}{28}$

13. $8\dfrac{3}{4} + 7\dfrac{3}{13} = 15\dfrac{51}{52}$
14. $2\dfrac{3}{5} + 3\dfrac{5}{6} = 6\dfrac{13}{30}$
15. $1\dfrac{3}{8} + 1\dfrac{1}{2} = 2\dfrac{7}{8}$

Total Problems _15_ Problems Correct ____

© Carson-Dellosa CD- 3749   23

Worksheet 24

Subtract. Write answers in simplest form.

1. $\dfrac{5}{6} - \dfrac{1}{6} = \dfrac{2}{3}$
2. $\dfrac{7}{8} - \dfrac{3}{8} = \dfrac{1}{2}$
3. $\dfrac{3}{10} - \dfrac{1}{10} = \dfrac{1}{5}$
4. $\dfrac{15}{16} - \dfrac{7}{16} = \dfrac{1}{2}$

5. $\dfrac{3}{4} - \dfrac{1}{4} = \dfrac{1}{2}$
6. $\dfrac{5}{7} - \dfrac{2}{7} = \dfrac{3}{7}$
7. $\dfrac{7}{9} - \dfrac{1}{9} = \dfrac{2}{3}$
8. $\dfrac{4}{5} - \dfrac{2}{5} = \dfrac{2}{5}$

9. $\dfrac{5}{9} - \dfrac{2}{9} = \dfrac{1}{3}$
10. $\dfrac{5}{8} - \dfrac{1}{8} = \dfrac{1}{2}$
11. $\dfrac{2}{3} - \dfrac{1}{3} = \dfrac{1}{3}$
12. $\dfrac{3}{6} - \dfrac{2}{6} = \dfrac{1}{6}$

13. $\dfrac{7}{8} - \dfrac{5}{8} = \dfrac{1}{4}$
14. $\dfrac{5}{9} - \dfrac{4}{9} = \dfrac{1}{9}$
15. $\dfrac{5}{7} - \dfrac{3}{7} = \dfrac{2}{7}$
16. $\dfrac{2}{5} - \dfrac{1}{5} = \dfrac{1}{5}$

17. $\dfrac{3}{7} - \dfrac{2}{7} = \dfrac{1}{7}$
18. $\dfrac{4}{6} - \dfrac{2}{6} = \dfrac{1}{3}$
19. $\dfrac{2}{3} - \dfrac{1}{3} = \dfrac{1}{3}$
20. $\dfrac{3}{4} - \dfrac{2}{4} = \dfrac{1}{4}$

Total Problems _20_ Problems Correct ____

© Carson-Dellosa CD-3749   24

Answer Key

Worksheet (page 25)

Name_____ Skill: Subtracting Fractions with the Same Denominators

Subtract. Write answers in simplest form.

1. $\frac{2}{5} - \frac{1}{5} = \frac{1}{5}$
2. $\frac{7}{8} - \frac{3}{8} = \frac{1}{2}$
3. $\frac{7}{10} - \frac{3}{10} = \frac{2}{5}$
4. $\frac{11}{14} - \frac{9}{14} = \frac{1}{7}$

5. $\frac{5}{7} - \frac{2}{7} = \frac{3}{7}$
6. $\frac{2}{3} - \frac{1}{3} = \frac{1}{3}$
7. $\frac{7}{8} - \frac{5}{8} = \frac{1}{4}$
8. $\frac{5}{6} - \frac{1}{6} = \frac{2}{3}$

9. $\frac{3}{5} - \frac{1}{5} = \frac{2}{5}$
10. $\frac{7}{9} - \frac{5}{9} = \frac{2}{9}$
11. $\frac{2}{3} - \frac{1}{3} = \frac{1}{3}$
12. $\frac{4}{5} - \frac{2}{5} = \frac{2}{5}$

13. $\frac{2}{8} - \frac{1}{8} = \frac{1}{8}$
14. $\frac{4}{6} - \frac{1}{6} = \frac{1}{2}$
15. $\frac{5}{9} - \frac{1}{9} = \frac{4}{9}$
16. $\frac{1}{2} - \frac{1}{2} = 0$

17. $\frac{2}{4} - \frac{1}{4} = \frac{1}{4}$
18. $\frac{4}{7} - \frac{2}{7} = \frac{2}{7}$
19. $\frac{4}{8} - \frac{1}{8} = \frac{3}{8}$
20. $\frac{3}{5} - \frac{2}{5} = \frac{1}{5}$

Total Problems _20_ Problems Correct ____

Worksheet (page 26)

Name_____ Skill: Subtracting Fractions with Different Denominators

Subtract. Write answers in simplest form.

1. $\frac{3}{9} - \frac{1}{4} = \frac{1}{12}$
2. $\frac{2}{3} - \frac{4}{9} = \frac{2}{9}$
3. $\frac{7}{12} - \frac{1}{4} = \frac{1}{3}$
4. $\frac{2}{3} - \frac{1}{2} = \frac{1}{6}$
5. $\frac{5}{6} - \frac{1}{5} = \frac{19}{30}$

6. $\frac{3}{4} - \frac{1}{5} = \frac{11}{20}$
7. $\frac{2}{6} - \frac{2}{8} = \frac{1}{12}$
8. $\frac{3}{9} - \frac{1}{4} = \frac{1}{12}$
9. $\frac{1}{2} - \frac{1}{4} = \frac{1}{4}$
10. $\frac{7}{8} - \frac{3}{10} = \frac{23}{40}$

11. $\frac{9}{10} - \frac{1}{2} = \frac{2}{5}$
12. $\frac{2}{4} - \frac{1}{3} = \frac{1}{6}$
13. $\frac{7}{8} - \frac{1}{9} = \frac{55}{72}$
14. $\frac{1}{3} - \frac{1}{6} = \frac{1}{6}$
15. $\frac{1}{5} - \frac{1}{8} = \frac{3}{40}$

16. $\frac{5}{7} - \frac{2}{9} = \frac{31}{63}$
17. $\frac{1}{5} - \frac{1}{8} = \frac{3}{40}$
18. $\frac{8}{8} - \frac{4}{6} = \frac{1}{3}$
19. $\frac{8}{9} - \frac{3}{6} = \frac{7}{18}$
20. $\frac{6}{6} - \frac{3}{12} = \frac{3}{4}$

Total Problems _20_ Problems Correct ____

Worksheet (page 27)

Name_____ Skill: Subtracting Fractions With Different Denominators

Subtract. Write answers in simplest form.

1. $\frac{3}{4} - \frac{1}{6} = \frac{7}{12}$
2. $\frac{5}{6} - \frac{2}{5} = \frac{13}{30}$
3. $\frac{11}{12} - \frac{1}{6} = \frac{3}{4}$
4. $\frac{5}{12} - \frac{1}{3} = \frac{1}{12}$
5. $\frac{3}{4} - \frac{1}{3} = \frac{5}{12}$

6. $\frac{13}{15} - \frac{2}{3} = \frac{1}{5}$
7. $\frac{2}{3} - \frac{1}{6} = \frac{1}{2}$
8. $\frac{5}{6} - \frac{3}{7} = \frac{17}{42}$
9. $\frac{7}{8} - \frac{1}{6} = \frac{17}{24}$
10. $\frac{8}{9} - \frac{5}{6} = \frac{1}{18}$

11. $\frac{2}{3} - \frac{7}{12} = \frac{1}{12}$
12. $\frac{11}{14} - \frac{1}{2} = \frac{2}{7}$
13. $\frac{7}{8} - \frac{1}{9} = \frac{55}{72}$
14. $\frac{1}{3} - \frac{1}{6} = \frac{1}{6}$
15. $\frac{3}{12} - \frac{1}{10} = \frac{3}{20}$

16. $\frac{5}{6} - \frac{1}{3} = \frac{1}{2}$
17. $\frac{7}{12} - \frac{1}{4} = \frac{1}{3}$
18. $\frac{7}{8} - \frac{1}{2} = \frac{3}{8}$
19. $\frac{2}{3} - \frac{4}{9} = \frac{2}{9}$
20. $\frac{5}{6} - \frac{1}{8} = \frac{17}{24}$

Total Problems _20_ Problems Correct ____

Worksheet (page 28)

Name_____ Skill: Subtracting Fractions from Whole Numbers

Subtract. Write answers in simplest form.

1. $2 - \frac{7}{8} = 1\frac{1}{8}$
2. $4 - \frac{2}{5} = 3\frac{3}{5}$
3. $5 - \frac{2}{3} = 4\frac{1}{3}$
4. $6 - \frac{1}{8} = 5\frac{7}{8}$

5. $3 - \frac{3}{4} = 2\frac{1}{4}$
6. $8 - \frac{9}{10} = 7\frac{1}{10}$
7. $7 - \frac{4}{5} = 6\frac{1}{5}$
8. $4 - \frac{3}{10} = 3\frac{7}{10}$

9. $5 - \frac{6}{9} = 4\frac{1}{3}$
10. $4 - \frac{2}{6} = 3\frac{2}{3}$
11. $5 - \frac{2}{5} = 4\frac{3}{5}$
12. $10 - \frac{1}{2} = 9\frac{1}{2}$

13. $12 - \frac{5}{7} = 11\frac{2}{7}$
14. $9 - \frac{1}{3} = 8\frac{2}{3}$
15. $4 - \frac{7}{8} = 3\frac{1}{8}$
16. $3 - \frac{6}{7} = 2\frac{1}{7}$

Total Problems _16_ Problems Correct ____

Answer Key

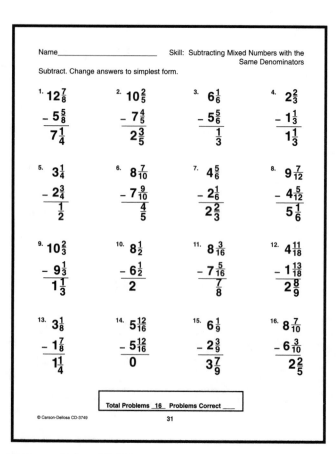

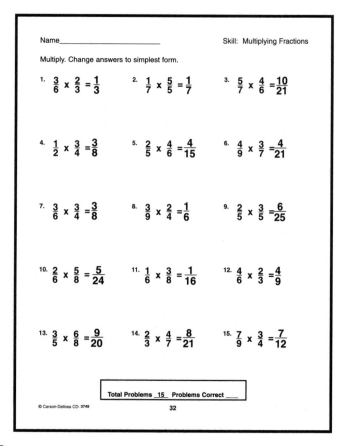

Page 29

Name_____   Skill: Subtracting Fractions from Whole Numbers

Subtract. Write answers in simplest form.

1. $15 - \frac{3}{8} = 14\frac{5}{8}$
2. $10 - \frac{2}{5} = 9\frac{3}{5}$
3. $1 - \frac{1}{3} = \frac{2}{3}$
4. $2 - \frac{6}{11} = 1\frac{5}{11}$

5. $5 - \frac{3}{5} = 4\frac{2}{5}$
6. $9 - \frac{3}{7} = 8\frac{4}{7}$
7. $14 - \frac{2}{9} = 13\frac{7}{9}$
8. $13 - \frac{2}{3} = 12\frac{1}{3}$

9. $1 - \frac{7}{8} = \frac{1}{8}$
10. $6 - \frac{1}{5} = 5\frac{4}{5}$
11. $7 - \frac{5}{6} = 6\frac{1}{6}$
12. $5 - \frac{1}{4} = 4\frac{3}{4}$

13. $8 - \frac{3}{4} = 7\frac{1}{4}$
14. $4 - \frac{1}{2} = 3\frac{1}{2}$
15. $2 - \frac{1}{6} = 1\frac{5}{6}$
16. $6 - \frac{3}{7} = 5\frac{4}{7}$

Total Problems _16_ Problems Correct ___

29

Page 30

Name_____   Skill: Subtracting Mixed Numbers With the Same Denominators

Subtract.

1. $8\frac{4}{5} - 1\frac{1}{5} = 7\frac{3}{5}$
2. $5\frac{2}{3} - 4\frac{1}{3} = 1\frac{1}{3}$
3. $3\frac{1}{2} - 1\frac{1}{2} = 2$
4. $4\frac{2}{6} - 3\frac{5}{6} = \frac{1}{2}$

5. $5\frac{3}{12} - 2\frac{2}{12} = 3\frac{1}{12}$
6. $3\frac{3}{5} - 1\frac{4}{5} = 1\frac{4}{5}$
7. $10\frac{1}{4} - 7\frac{1}{4} = 3$
8. $6\frac{7}{8} - 1\frac{1}{8} = 5\frac{3}{4}$

9. $5\frac{1}{3} - 4\frac{2}{3} = \frac{2}{3}$
10. $5\frac{3}{8} - 3\frac{3}{8} = 2$
11. $9\frac{6}{7} - 2\frac{2}{7} = 7\frac{4}{7}$
12. $2\frac{1}{8} - 1\frac{1}{8} = 1$

13. $7\frac{3}{8} - 5\frac{1}{8} = 2\frac{1}{4}$
14. $4\frac{11}{13} - 2\frac{12}{13} = 1\frac{12}{13}$
15. $7\frac{1}{6} - 5\frac{5}{6} = 1\frac{2}{3}$
16. $3\frac{7}{9} - 2\frac{2}{9} = 1\frac{2}{3}$

Total Problems _16_ Problems Correct ___

30

Page 31

Name_____   Skill: Subtracting Mixed Numbers with the Same Denominators

Subtract. Change answers to simplest form.

1. $12\frac{7}{8} - 5\frac{5}{8} = 7\frac{1}{4}$
2. $10\frac{2}{5} - 7\frac{4}{5} = 2\frac{3}{5}$
3. $6\frac{1}{6} - 5\frac{5}{6} = \frac{1}{3}$
4. $2\frac{2}{3} - 1\frac{1}{3} = 1\frac{1}{3}$

5. $3\frac{1}{4} - 2\frac{3}{4} = \frac{1}{2}$
6. $8\frac{7}{10} - 7\frac{9}{10} = \frac{4}{5}$
7. $4\frac{5}{6} - 2\frac{1}{6} = 2\frac{2}{3}$
8. $9\frac{7}{12} - 4\frac{5}{12} = 5\frac{1}{6}$

9. $10\frac{2}{3} - 9\frac{1}{3} = 1\frac{1}{3}$
10. $8\frac{1}{2} - 6\frac{1}{2} = 2$
11. $8\frac{3}{16} - 7\frac{5}{16} = \frac{7}{8}$
12. $4\frac{11}{18} - 1\frac{13}{18} = 2\frac{8}{9}$

13. $3\frac{1}{8} - 1\frac{7}{8} = 1\frac{1}{4}$
14. $5\frac{12}{16} - 5\frac{12}{16} = 0$
15. $6\frac{1}{9} - 2\frac{3}{9} = 3\frac{7}{9}$
16. $8\frac{7}{10} - 6\frac{3}{10} = 2\frac{2}{5}$

Total Problems _16_ Problems Correct ___

31

Page 32

Name_____   Skill: Multiplying Fractions

Multiply. Change answers to simplest form.

1. $\frac{3}{6} \times \frac{2}{3} = \frac{1}{3}$
2. $\frac{1}{7} \times \frac{5}{5} = \frac{1}{7}$
3. $\frac{5}{7} \times \frac{4}{6} = \frac{10}{21}$

4. $\frac{1}{2} \times \frac{3}{4} = \frac{3}{8}$
5. $\frac{2}{5} \times \frac{4}{6} = \frac{4}{15}$
6. $\frac{4}{9} \times \frac{3}{7} = \frac{4}{21}$

7. $\frac{3}{6} \times \frac{3}{4} = \frac{3}{8}$
8. $\frac{3}{9} \times \frac{2}{4} = \frac{1}{6}$
9. $\frac{2}{5} \times \frac{3}{5} = \frac{6}{25}$

10. $\frac{2}{6} \times \frac{5}{8} = \frac{5}{24}$
11. $\frac{1}{6} \times \frac{3}{8} = \frac{1}{16}$
12. $\frac{4}{6} \times \frac{2}{3} = \frac{4}{9}$

13. $\frac{3}{5} \times \frac{6}{8} = \frac{9}{20}$
14. $\frac{2}{3} \times \frac{4}{7} = \frac{8}{21}$
15. $\frac{7}{9} \times \frac{3}{4} = \frac{7}{12}$

Total Problems _15_ Problems Correct ___

32

Answer Key

Name_____   Skill: Multiplying Fractions

Multiply. Change answers to simplest form.

1. $\frac{3}{5} \times \frac{2}{6} = \frac{1}{5}$
2. $\frac{2}{4} \times \frac{3}{7} = \frac{3}{14}$
3. $\frac{1}{9} \times \frac{3}{6} = \frac{1}{18}$

4. $\frac{3}{9} \times \frac{2}{5} = \frac{2}{15}$
5. $\frac{3}{8} \times \frac{5}{6} = \frac{5}{16}$
6. $\frac{4}{7} \times \frac{3}{8} = \frac{3}{14}$

7. $\frac{4}{6} \times \frac{2}{5} = \frac{4}{15}$
8. $\frac{3}{4} \times \frac{2}{3} = \frac{1}{2}$
9. $\frac{2}{5} \times \frac{6}{8} = \frac{3}{10}$

10. $\frac{2}{4} \times \frac{1}{6} = \frac{1}{12}$
11. $\frac{3}{5} \times \frac{7}{8} = \frac{21}{40}$
12. $\frac{1}{4} \times \frac{1}{5} = \frac{1}{20}$

13. $\frac{2}{7} \times \frac{4}{5} = \frac{8}{35}$
14. $\frac{3}{6} \times \frac{1}{6} = \frac{1}{12}$
15. $\frac{1}{3} \times \frac{4}{7} = \frac{4}{21}$

Total Problems __15__ Problems Correct ____

33

Name_____   Skill: Multiplying Fractions and Whole Numbers

Multiply. Write answers in simplest form.

1. $5 \times \frac{2}{5} = 2$
2. $\frac{2}{3} \times 4 = 2\frac{2}{3}$
3. $\frac{3}{4} \times 5 = 3\frac{3}{4}$

4. $8 \times \frac{1}{7} = 1\frac{1}{7}$
5. $\frac{1}{9} \times 6 = \frac{2}{3}$
6. $2 \times \frac{4}{5} = 1\frac{3}{5}$

7. $6 \times \frac{3}{8} = 2\frac{1}{4}$
8. $\frac{5}{6} \times 4 = 3\frac{1}{3}$
9. $\frac{2}{7} \times 6 = 1\frac{5}{7}$

10. $4 \times \frac{8}{9} = 3\frac{5}{9}$
11. $\frac{4}{6} \times 3 = 2$
12. $7 \times \frac{3}{5} = 4\frac{1}{5}$

13. $2 \times \frac{3}{7} = \frac{6}{7}$
14. $\frac{4}{5} \times 6 = 4\frac{4}{5}$
15. $7 \times \frac{5}{6} = 5\frac{5}{6}$

Total Problems __15__ Problems Correct ____

34

Name_____   Skill: Multiplying Fractions and Whole Numbers

Multiply. Change answers to simplest form.

1. $4 \times \frac{1}{2} = 2$
2. $\frac{2}{5} \times 3 = 1\frac{1}{5}$
3. $\frac{1}{3} \times 7 = 2\frac{1}{3}$

4. $2 \times \frac{2}{5} = \frac{4}{5}$
5. $\frac{1}{8} \times 5 = \frac{5}{8}$
6. $4 \times \frac{3}{4} = 3$

7. $4 \times \frac{2}{7} = 1\frac{1}{7}$
8. $\frac{5}{7} \times 5 = 3\frac{4}{7}$
9. $\frac{6}{8} \times 2 = 1\frac{1}{2}$

10. $3 \times \frac{5}{6} = 2\frac{1}{2}$
11. $\frac{2}{3} \times 2 = 1\frac{1}{3}$
12. $5 \times \frac{4}{5} = 4$

13. $8 \times \frac{1}{8} = 1$
14. $\frac{3}{9} \times 4 = 1\frac{1}{3}$
15. $3 \times \frac{2}{3} = 2$

Total Problems __15__ Problems Correct ____

35

Name_____   Skill: Multiplying Mixed Numbers and Whole Numbers

Multiply. Change answers to simplest form.

1. $4 \times 3\frac{3}{5} = 14\frac{2}{5}$
2. $10 \times 5\frac{1}{2} = 55$
3. $2 \times 5\frac{1}{8} = 10\frac{1}{4}$

4. $6 \times 9\frac{4}{5} = 58\frac{4}{5}$
5. $8 \times 2\frac{3}{8} = 19$
6. $3 \times 1\frac{15}{16} = 5\frac{13}{16}$

7. $2 \times 8\frac{3}{4} = 17\frac{1}{2}$
8. $5 \times 4\frac{2}{5} = 22$
9. $4 \times 8\frac{6}{7} = 35\frac{3}{7}$

10. $9 \times 1\frac{1}{18} = 9\frac{1}{2}$
11. $2 \times 7\frac{5}{8} = 15\frac{1}{4}$
12. $2 \times 2\frac{1}{4} = 4\frac{1}{2}$

Total Problems __12__ Problems Correct ____

36

Answer Key

Name_____   Skill: Multiplying Mixed Numbers
                                              and Whole Numbers

Multiply. Change answers to simplest form.

1. $2 \times 2\frac{1}{3} = 4\frac{2}{3}$ 2. $4 \times 5\frac{1}{8} = 20\frac{1}{2}$ 3. $7 \times 1\frac{3}{4} = 12\frac{1}{4}$

4. $3 \times 5\frac{1}{5} = 15\frac{3}{5}$ 5. $6 \times 3\frac{1}{6} = 19$ 6. $7 \times 2\frac{3}{5} = 18\frac{1}{5}$

7. $9 \times 3\frac{2}{3} = 33$ 8. $5 \times 6\frac{5}{8} = 33\frac{1}{8}$ 9. $4 \times 2\frac{1}{2} = 10$

10. $8 \times 9\frac{1}{10} = 7\frac{4}{5}$ 11. $3 \times 9\frac{1}{3} = 28$ 12. $7 \times 2\frac{1}{7} = 15$

Total Problems _12_ Problems Correct ____

© Carson-Dellosa CD-3749
37

Name_____   Skill: Dividing Fractions

Divide. Write answers in simplest form.

1. $\frac{3}{4} \div \frac{5}{6} = \frac{9}{10}$ 2. $\frac{3}{16} \div \frac{3}{8} = \frac{1}{2}$ 3. $\frac{7}{9} \div \frac{2}{3} = 1\frac{1}{6}$

4. $\frac{5}{8} \div \frac{3}{5} = 1\frac{1}{24}$ 5. $\frac{4}{9} \div \frac{3}{4} = \frac{16}{27}$ 6. $\frac{7}{8} \div \frac{5}{11} = 1\frac{37}{40}$

7. $\frac{7}{10} \div \frac{3}{5} = 1\frac{1}{6}$ 8. $\frac{7}{8} \div \frac{2}{3} = 1\frac{5}{16}$ 9. $\frac{2}{5} \div \frac{3}{8} = 1\frac{1}{15}$

10. $\frac{4}{7} \div \frac{3}{7} = 1\frac{1}{3}$ 11. $\frac{1}{6} \div \frac{4}{5} = \frac{5}{24}$ 12. $\frac{2}{3} \div \frac{4}{5} = \frac{5}{6}$

13. $\frac{3}{5} \div \frac{7}{8} = \frac{24}{35}$ 14. $\frac{3}{4} \div \frac{3}{5} = 1\frac{1}{4}$ 15. $\frac{9}{16} \div \frac{3}{4} = \frac{3}{4}$

Total Problems _15_ Problems Correct ____

© Carson-Dellosa CD-3749
38

Name_____   Skill: Dividing Fractions

Divide. Write answers in simplest form.

1. $\frac{1}{2} \div \frac{7}{8} = \frac{4}{7}$ 2. $\frac{6}{11} \div \frac{3}{8} = 1\frac{5}{11}$ 3. $\frac{7}{9} \div \frac{2}{5} = 1\frac{17}{18}$

4. $\frac{5}{6} \div \frac{1}{5} = 4\frac{1}{6}$ 5. $\frac{3}{4} \div \frac{3}{4} = 1$ 6. $\frac{7}{8} \div \frac{5}{12} = 2\frac{1}{10}$

7. $\frac{7}{13} \div \frac{4}{5} = \frac{35}{52}$ 8. $\frac{11}{12} \div \frac{2}{9} = 4\frac{1}{8}$ 9. $\frac{2}{3} \div \frac{3}{8} = 1\frac{7}{9}$

10. $\frac{4}{7} \div \frac{4}{5} = \frac{5}{7}$ 11. $\frac{1}{8} \div \frac{3}{5} = \frac{5}{24}$ 12. $\frac{2}{5} \div \frac{2}{7} = 1\frac{2}{5}$

13. $\frac{3}{8} \div \frac{5}{9} = \frac{27}{40}$ 14. $\frac{1}{4} \div \frac{3}{7} = \frac{7}{12}$ 15. $\frac{9}{17} \div \frac{1}{4} = 2\frac{2}{17}$

Total Problems _15_ Problems Correct ____

© Carson-Dellosa CD-3749
39

Name_____   Skill: Dividing Fractions and
                                              Whole Numbers

Divide. Write answers in simplest form.

1. $8 \div \frac{6}{7} = 9\frac{1}{3}$ 2. $\frac{5}{6} \div 10 = \frac{1}{12}$ 3. $\frac{2}{5} \div 3 = \frac{2}{15}$

4. $3 \div \frac{1}{2} = 6$ 5. $\frac{2}{3} \div 6 = \frac{1}{9}$ 6. $10 \div \frac{6}{7} = 11\frac{2}{3}$

7. $12 \div \frac{3}{4} = 16$ 8. $\frac{3}{4} \div 4 = \frac{3}{16}$ 9. $\frac{4}{7} \div 5 = \frac{4}{35}$

10. $14 \div \frac{7}{8} = 16$ 11. $\frac{1}{2} \div 6 = \frac{1}{12}$ 12. $6 \div \frac{1}{5} = 30$

13. $8 \div \frac{1}{2} = 16$ 14. $\frac{1}{4} \div 2 = \frac{1}{8}$ 15. $9 \div \frac{1}{3} = 27$

Total Problems _15_ Problems Correct ____

© Carson-Dellosa CD-3749
40

Answer Key

Name_____ Skill: Dividing Fractions and
Whole Numbers

Divide. Write answers in simplest form.

1. $5 \div \frac{6}{8} = 6\frac{2}{3}$ 2. $\frac{5}{5} \div 12 = \frac{1}{12}$ 3. $\frac{2}{3} \div 3 = \frac{2}{9}$

4. $2 \div \frac{3}{7} = 4\frac{2}{3}$ 5. $\frac{2}{5} \div 3 = \frac{2}{15}$ 6. $8 \div \frac{3}{5} = 13\frac{1}{3}$

7. $6 \div \frac{5}{6} = 7\frac{1}{5}$ 8. $\frac{3}{8} \div 3 = \frac{1}{8}$ 9. $\frac{4}{5} \div 2 = \frac{2}{5}$

10. $12 \div \frac{1}{2} = 24$ 11. $\frac{1}{2} \div 5 = \frac{1}{10}$ 12. $5 \div \frac{1}{5} = 25$

13. $3 \div \frac{1}{6} = 18$ 14. $\frac{1}{4} \div 4 = \frac{1}{16}$ 15. $8 \div \frac{1}{3} = 24$

Total Problems _15_ Problems Correct ____

41

Name_____ Skill: Dividing Mixed Numbers
and Fractions

Divide. Write answers in simplest form.

1. $1\frac{1}{6} \div \frac{1}{4} = 4\frac{2}{3}$ 2. $2\frac{3}{4} \div \frac{1}{8} = 22$ 3. $6\frac{1}{8} \div \frac{4}{7} = 10\frac{23}{32}$

4. $3\frac{1}{4} \div \frac{3}{8} = 8\frac{2}{3}$ 5. $2\frac{1}{2} \div \frac{1}{2} = 5$ 6. $2\frac{3}{4} \div \frac{1}{2} = 5\frac{1}{2}$

7. $5\frac{2}{3} \div \frac{9}{10} = 6\frac{8}{27}$ 8. $2\frac{1}{4} \div \frac{3}{8} = 6$ 9. $1\frac{1}{4} \div \frac{2}{3} = 1\frac{7}{8}$

10. $1\frac{4}{5} \div \frac{2}{7} = 6\frac{3}{10}$ 11. $4\frac{1}{2} \div \frac{1}{2} = 9$ 12. $1\frac{2}{5} \div \frac{1}{3} = 4\frac{1}{5}$

Total Problems _12_ Problems Correct ____

42

Name_____ Skill: Dividing Mixed Numbers
and Fractions

Divide. Write answers in simplest form.

1. $1\frac{1}{6} \div \frac{1}{4} = 4\frac{2}{3}$ 2. $3\frac{1}{2} \div \frac{1}{4} = 14$ 3. $1\frac{1}{3} \div \frac{3}{8} = 3\frac{5}{9}$

4. $2\frac{2}{5} \div \frac{2}{3} = 3\frac{3}{5}$ 5. $5\frac{1}{3} \div \frac{3}{8} = 14\frac{2}{9}$ 6. $3\frac{3}{5} \div 10 = \frac{9}{25}$

7. $6\frac{3}{8} \div \frac{7}{10} = 9\frac{3}{28}$ 8. $3\frac{1}{3} \div \frac{3}{4} = 4\frac{4}{9}$ 9. $1\frac{1}{5} \div \frac{2}{5} = 3$

10. $1\frac{1}{3} \div \frac{7}{8} = 1\frac{11}{21}$ 11. $2\frac{1}{3} \div 5 = \frac{7}{15}$ 12. $5\frac{6}{7} \div \frac{3}{4} = 7\frac{17}{21}$

Total Problems _12_ Problems Correct ____

43

Name_____ Skill: Making Fractions Equivalent

Make the following fractions equivalent.

1. $\frac{1}{2} = \frac{2}{4}$ 2. $\frac{3}{4} = \frac{9}{12}$ 3. $\frac{1}{4} = \frac{2}{8}$ 4. $\frac{1}{3} = \frac{3}{9}$ 5. $\frac{2}{5} = \frac{6}{15}$

6. $\frac{3}{5} = \frac{12}{20}$ 7. $\frac{2}{3} = \frac{8}{12}$ 8. $\frac{2}{7} = \frac{4}{14}$ 9. $\frac{2}{3} = \frac{6}{9}$ 10. $\frac{3}{4} = \frac{9}{12}$

11. $\frac{5}{6} = \frac{35}{42}$ 12. $\frac{1}{5} = \frac{5}{25}$ 13. $\frac{3}{7} = \frac{12}{28}$ 14. $\frac{1}{8} = \frac{8}{64}$ 15. $\frac{1}{6} = \frac{5}{30}$

Complete each row to make each fraction equal to the first one.

16. $\frac{1}{2} = \frac{3}{6} = \frac{4}{8} = \frac{6}{12} = \frac{2}{4} = \frac{5}{10}$

17. $\frac{2}{3} = \frac{8}{12} = \frac{4}{6} = \frac{10}{15} = \frac{6}{9} = \frac{12}{18}$

18. $\frac{1}{4} = \frac{2}{8} = \frac{5}{20} = \frac{3}{12} = \frac{6}{24} = \frac{4}{16}$

19. $\frac{3}{5} = \frac{15}{25} = \frac{9}{15} = \frac{6}{10} = \frac{12}{20} = \frac{18}{30}$

Total Problems _19_ Problems Correct ____

44

Answer Key

Worksheet 45 — Skill: Adding Decimals

Name_____

Add.

1. $2.4 + 1.7 = 4.1$
2. $8.1 + 9.2 = 17.3$
3. $10.3 + 7.4 = 17.7$
4. $1.5 + 1.5 = 3$
5. $18.6 + 9.5 = 28.1$
6. $14.3 + 1.9 = 16.2$
7. $24.7 + 32.6 = 57.3$
8. $20.5 + 32.3 = 52.8$
9. $.01 + .72 = .73$
10. $1.04 + 2.07 = 3.11$
11. $16.52 + 13.63 = 30.15$
12. $14.87 + 56.09 = 70.96$
13. $3.2 + 1.4 + 7.8 = 12.4$
14. $86.7 + 5.2 + 8.4 = 100.3$
15. $9.1 + 12.5 + 19.4 = 41.0$
16. $40.08 + 60.27 + 50.33 = 150.68$
17. $2.016 + 3.094 + 8.627 = 13.737$
18. $42.65 + 87.61 + 12.12 = 142.38$
19. $492.6 + 382.3 + 225.7 = 1{,}100.6$
20. $4.008 + 1.318 + .056 = 5.382$

Total Problems 20   Problems Correct ____

45

Worksheet 46 — Skill: Adding Decimals

Name_____

Add.

1. $2.34 + .02 + 1.65 = 4.01$
2. $22.87 + 45.7 + 1.26 = 69.83$
3. $.605 + 1.70 + 23.75 = 26.055$
4. $.2 + 1.2 + .12 = 1.52$
5. $543.7 + 3.42 + .06 = 547.18$
6. $987.5 + 1.4 + 30.2 = 1{,}019.1$
7. $86.15 + .07 + 5.72 = 91.94$
8. $1.45 + 20.03 + .17 = 21.65$
9. $72.56 + 12.38 + .07 = 85.01$
10. $2.14 + .007 + 72.4 = 74.547$
11. $5.1 + 7.53 + 87.4 = 100.03$
12. $4.5 + 5.4 + 12.67 = 22.57$
13. $42.7 + .03 + 1.7 = 44.43$
14. $.725 + 1.33 + 12 = 14.055$
15. $87.5 + 1.2 + 591.35 = 680.05$
16. $42 + .543 + 7.8 = 50.343$

Total Problems 16   Problems Correct ____

46

Worksheet 47 — Skill: Subtracting Decimals

Name_____

Subtract.

1. $19.867 - 1.070 = 18.797$
2. $20.342 - .67 = 19.672$
3. $1.428 - 1.2 = .228$
4. $32.456 - 1.2 = 31.256$
5. $4.52 - .4 = 4.12$
6. $756.83 - 22.5 = 734.33$
7. $71.34 - 2.672 = 68.668$
8. $81.384 - 2.777 = 78.607$
9. $4.254 - 3.01 = 1.244$
10. $38.7 - 5.21 = 33.49$
11. $31.1 - 3.052 = 28.048$
12. $24.75 - 6.243 = 18.507$
13. $23.154 - 3.08 = 20.074$
14. $.65 - .224 = .426$
15. $.7 - .506 = .194$
16. $2.3 - 1.437 = .863$

Total Problems 16   Problems Correct ____

47

Worksheet 48 — Skill: Subtracting Decimals

Name_____

Subtract.

1. $.8 - .3 = .5$
2. $.9 - .4 = .5$
3. $.3 - .2 = .1$
4. $.6 - .2 = .4$
5. $.47 - .21 = .26$
6. $.27 - .25 = .02$
7. $.22 - .15 = .07$
8. $.40 - .11 = .29$
9. $.741 - .215 = .526$
10. $.833 - .501 = .332$
11. $.428 - .338 = .09$
12. $.575 - .104 = .471$
13. $4.6 - 2.1 = 2.5$
14. $3.6 - .2 = 3.4$
15. $39.6 - .7 = 38.9$
16. $36.06 - 3.72 = 32.34$
17. $40.15 - .22 = 39.93$
18. $86.33 - 6.21 = 80.12$
19. $85.43 - 15.07 = 70.36$
20. $52.27 - 5.41 = 46.86$

Total Problems 20   Problems Correct ____

48

Answer Key

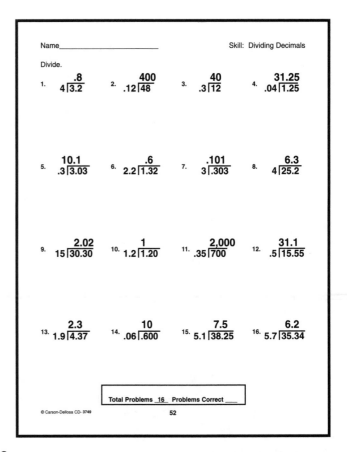

Answer Key

Name_____ Skill: Changing Fractions and Mixed
Numbers to Decimals

Change the following fractions or mixed numbers to decimals.

1. $\frac{1}{4}$ = .25   2. $\frac{2}{5}$ = .4   3. $\frac{49}{50}$ = .98   4. $\frac{17}{10}$ = 1.7   5. $\frac{1}{5}$ = .2

6. $\frac{7}{50}$ = .14   7. $\frac{2}{10}$ = .2   8. $\frac{31}{50}$ = .62   9. $\frac{13}{50}$ = .26   10. $\frac{9}{10}$ = .9

11. $\frac{3}{5}$ = .6   12. $\frac{3}{4}$ = .75   13. $\frac{7}{20}$ = .35   14. $\frac{7}{25}$ = .28   15. $\frac{3}{10}$ = .3

16. $1\frac{2}{5}$ = 1.4   17. $3\frac{31}{50}$ = 3.62   18. $1\frac{43}{50}$ = 1.86   19. $4\frac{4}{25}$ = 4.16

20. $4\frac{4}{8}$ = 4.5   21. $5\frac{1}{5}$ = 5.2   22. $4\frac{1}{4}$ = 4.25   23. $2\frac{8}{32}$ = 2.25

Total Problems _23_ Problems Correct ____

53

Name_____ Skill: Changing Fractions and Mixed
Numbers to Decimals

Change the following fractions or mixed numbers to decimals.

1. $\frac{3}{5}$ = .6   2. $\frac{3}{10}$ = .3   3. $\frac{3}{6}$ = .5   4. $\frac{4}{5}$ = .8

5. $\frac{1}{8}$ = .125   6. $\frac{1}{10}$ = .1   7. $\frac{7}{8}$ = .875   8. $\frac{11}{20}$ = .55

9. $\frac{2}{8}$ = .25   10. $\frac{12}{25}$ = .48   11. $\frac{1}{4}$ = .25   12. $\frac{11}{25}$ = .44

13. $5\frac{6}{12}$ = 5.5   14. $4\frac{12}{24}$ = 4.5   15. $1\frac{4}{5}$ = 1.8

16. $5\frac{2}{5}$ = 5.4   17. $4\frac{15}{30}$ = 4.5   18. $6\frac{7}{8}$ = 6.875

Total Problems _18_ Problems Correct ____

54

Name_____ Skill: Changing Decimals to Fractions

Change each decimal to a fraction. Change to simplest form when possible.

1. .25 = $\frac{1}{4}$ 2. .05 = $\frac{1}{20}$ 3. .12 = $\frac{3}{25}$ 4. .88 = $\frac{22}{25}$

5. .015 = $\frac{3}{200}$ 6. .250 = $\frac{1}{4}$ 7. .02 = $\frac{1}{50}$ 8. .15 = $\frac{3}{20}$

9. .75 = $\frac{3}{4}$ 10. .35 = $\frac{7}{20}$ 11. .125 = $\frac{1}{8}$ 12. .825 = $\frac{33}{40}$

13. .18 = $\frac{9}{50}$ 14. .60 = $\frac{3}{5}$ 15. .20 = $\frac{1}{5}$ 16. .225 = $\frac{9}{40}$

Total Problems _16_ Problems Correct ____

55

Name_____ Skill: Changing Decimals to Fractions

Change each decimal to a fraction or mixed number.

1. .008 = $\frac{2}{250}$ 2. .018 = $\frac{9}{500}$ 3. .921 = $\frac{921}{1,000}$ 4. .4 = $\frac{2}{5}$

5. .45 = $\frac{9}{20}$ 6. .16 = $\frac{4}{25}$ 7. .155 = $\frac{31}{200}$ 8. .032 = $\frac{4}{125}$

9. 2.2 = $2\frac{1}{5}$ 10. 4.05 = $4\frac{1}{20}$ 11. 4.62 = $4\frac{31}{50}$ 12. 6.25 = $6\frac{1}{4}$

13. 3.024 = $3\frac{3}{125}$ 14. .12 = $\frac{3}{25}$ 15. .018 = $\frac{9}{500}$ 16. 3.25 = $3\frac{1}{4}$

Total Problems _16_ Problems Correct ____

56

Answer Key

Name_____ Skill: Changing Percentages to Fractions

Change the percentages to fractions. Change to simplest form when possible.

1. $20\% = \frac{1}{5}$ 2. $25\% = \frac{1}{4}$ 3. $30\% = \frac{3}{10}$ 4. $50\% = \frac{1}{2}$

5. $75\% = \frac{3}{4}$ 6. $22\% = \frac{11}{50}$ 7. $10\% = \frac{1}{10}$ 8. $4\% = \frac{1}{25}$

9. $15\% = \frac{3}{20}$ 10. $80\% = \frac{4}{5}$ 11. $27\% = \frac{27}{100}$ 12. $200\% = 2$

13. $31\% = \frac{31}{100}$ 14. $125\% = 1\frac{1}{4}$ 15. $85\% = \frac{17}{20}$ 16. $175\% = 1\frac{3}{4}$

Total Problems _16_ Problems Correct ____

57

Name_____ Skill: Changing Percentages to Fractions

Change the percentages to fractions. Change to simplest form when possible.

1. $44\% = \frac{11}{25}$ 2. $88\% = \frac{22}{25}$ 3. $25\% = \frac{1}{4}$ 4. $80\% = \frac{4}{5}$

5. $65\% = \frac{13}{20}$ 6. $78\% = \frac{39}{50}$ 7. $24\% = \frac{6}{25}$ 8. $42\% = \frac{21}{50}$

9. $10\% = \frac{1}{10}$ 10. $18\% = \frac{9}{50}$ 11. $45\% = \frac{9}{20}$ 12. $70\% = \frac{7}{10}$

13. $56\% = \frac{14}{25}$ 14. $15\% = \frac{3}{20}$ 15. $11\% = \frac{11}{100}$ 16. $120\% = 1\frac{1}{5}$

Total Problems _16_ Problems Correct ____

58

Name_____ Skill: Changing Percentages to Fractions

Change the percentages to fractions. Change to simplest form when possible.

1. $144\% = 1\frac{11}{25}$ 2. $65\% = \frac{13}{20}$ 3. $38\% = \frac{19}{50}$ 4. $55\% = \frac{11}{20}$

5. $25\% = \frac{1}{4}$ 6. $32\% = \frac{8}{25}$ 7. $12\% = \frac{3}{25}$ 8. $42\% = \frac{21}{50}$

9. $100\% = 1$ 10. $90\% = \frac{9}{10}$ 11. $47\% = \frac{47}{100}$ 12. $800\% = 8$

13. $15\% = \frac{3}{20}$ 14. $22\% = \frac{11}{50}$ 15. $13\% = \frac{13}{100}$ 16. $205\% = 2\frac{1}{20}$

Total Problems _16_ Problems Correct ____

59

Name_____ Skill: Changing Percentages to Fractions

Change the following percentages to fractions.

1. $20\% = \frac{1}{5}$ 2. $31\% = \frac{31}{100}$ 3. $28\% = \frac{7}{25}$ 4. $10\% = \frac{1}{10}$

5. $5\% = \frac{1}{20}$ 6. $18\% = \frac{9}{50}$ 7. $22\% = \frac{11}{50}$ 8. $88\% = \frac{22}{25}$

9. $77\% = \frac{77}{100}$ 10. $12\% = \frac{3}{25}$ 11. $30\% = \frac{3}{10}$ 12. $20\% = \frac{1}{5}$

13. $9\% = \frac{9}{100}$ 14. $11\% = \frac{11}{100}$ 15. $6\% = \frac{3}{50}$ 16. $188\% = 1\frac{22}{25}$

Total Problems _16_ Problems Correct ____

60

110

Answer Key

Name_____   Skill: Changing Percentages to Decimals

Change each percentage to a decimal.

1. 160% = **1.6** 2. 45% = **.45** 3. 28% = **.28** 4. 90% = **.9**

5. 37% = **.37** 6. 26% = **.26** 7. 89% = **.89** 8. 51% = **.51**

9. 300% = **3** 10. 20% = **.2** 11. 77% = **.77** 12. 132% = **1.32**

13. 45% = **.45** 14. 64% = **.64** 15. 79% = **.79** 16. 635% = **6.35**

Total Problems **16** Problems Correct ____

61

Name_____   Skill: Changing Percentages to Decimals

Change each percentage to a decimal.

1. 90% = **.9** 2. 21% = **.21** 3. 46% = **.46** 4. 79% = **.79**

5. 9% = **.09** 6. 75% = **.75** 7. 18% = **.18** 8. 44% = **.44**

9. 33% = **.33** 10. 19% = **.19** 11. 25% = **.25** 12. 80% = **.8**

13. 2% = **.02** 14. 29% = **.29** 15. 1% = **.01** 16. 456% = **4.56**

Total Problems **16** Problems Correct ____

62

Name_____   Skill: Fractions, Decimals, and Percentages Review

Complete the chart below.

	Fraction	Decimal	Percentage
1.	$4\frac{4}{5}$	4.8	480%
2.	$\frac{3}{4}$	.75	75%
3.	$\frac{7}{20}$	.35	35%
4.	$\frac{1}{5}$	.20	20%
5.	$\frac{7}{25}$	.28	28%
6.	$3\frac{3}{4}$	3.75	375%
7.	$2\frac{1}{5}$	2.2	220%
8.	$3\frac{7}{10}$	3.7	370%
9.	$\frac{9}{10}$	.9	90%

Total Problems **9** Problems Correct ____

63

Name_____   Skill: Finding Percentages

Solve. Write your answers in simplest form.

1. 8% of 200 = **16** 2. 5% of 80 = **4**

3. 15% of 210 = **31.5** 4. 25% of 216 = **54**

5. 5% of 95 = **4.75** 6. 50% of 32 = **16**

7. 80% of 75 = **60** 8. 90% of 12 = **10.8**

9. 14% of 65 = **9.1** 10. 22% of 87 = **19.14**

11. 61% of 45 = **27.45** 12. 74% of 50 = **37**

13. 16% of 110 = **17.6** 14. 50% of 87 = **43.5**

Total Problems **14** Problems Correct ____

64

111

Answer Key

Name_____
Skill: Finding Percentages

Find the percentages. Write your answers in simplest form.

1. 50% of 125 = __62.5__
2. 15% of 342 = __51.3__
3. 47% of 70 = __32.9__
4. 10% of 14 = __1.4__
5. 15% of 60 = __9__
6. 25% of 350 = __87.5__
7. 15% of 48 = __7.2__
8. 30% of 10 = __3__
9. 20% of 96 = __19.2__
10. 12% of 80 = __9.6__
11. 75% of 340 = __255__
12. 45% of 30 = __13.5__
13. 10% of 962 = __96.2__
14. 4% of 280 = __11.2__

Total Problems _14_ Problems Correct ____

© Carson-Dellosa CD- 3749
65

Name_____
Skill: Finding Percentages

Solve.

1. 50% of 220 = __110__
2. 12% of 144 = __17.28__
3. 42% of 30 = __12.6__
4. 12% of 18 = __2.16__
5. 15% of 60 = __9__
6. 20% of 300 = __60__
7. 25% of 40 = __10__
8. 34% of 14 = __4.76__
9. 80% of 100 = __80__
10. 17% of 7 = __1.19__
11. 65% of 300 = __195__
12. 35% of 50 = __17.5__
13. 12% of 802 = __96.24__
14. 6% of 110 = __6.6__

Total Problems _14_ Problems Correct ____

© Carson-Dellosa CD- 3749
66

Name_____
Skill: Finding Percentages

Solve. Round to the nearest tenth.

1. 25 is __25__ % of 100
2. 80 is __200__ % of 40
3. 32 is __21.3__ % of 150
4. 90 is __81.8__ % of 110
5. 27 is __54__ % of 50
6. 48 is __48.9__ % of 98
7. 36 is __60__ % of 60
8. 50 is __15.4__ % of 325
9. 18 is __4.19__ % of 430
10. 2 is __7.69__ % of 26
11. 13 is __25__ % of 52
12. 8 is __3.56__ % of 225
13. 5 is __35.7__ % of 14
14. 10 is __10__ % of 100

Total Problems _14_ Problems Correct ____

© Carson-Dellosa CD- 3749
67

Name_____
Skill: Finding Percentages

Solve.

1. 63 is __90__ % of 70
2. 21 is __30__ % of 70
3. 168 is __152.7__ % of 110
4. 24 is __40__ % of 60
5. 90 is __125__ % of 72
6. 18 is __60__ % of 30
7. 903 is __215__ % of 420
8. 225 is __150__ % of 150
9. 18 is __4.19__ % of 430
10. 2 is __7.69__ % of 26
11. 8 is __40__ % of 20
12. 5 is __125__ % of 4
13. 20 is __250__ % of 8
14. 9 is __7.5__ % of 120

Total Problems _14_ Problems Correct ____

© Carson-Dellosa CD- 3749
68

Answer Key

Name_____   Skill: Finding Percentages

Solve. Round to the nearest tenth.

1. 18 is 90% of __20__

2. 25 is 30% of __83.3__

3. 47 is 20% of __235__

4. 10 is 40% of __25__

5. 55 is 34% of __161.7__

6. 35 is 125% of __28__

7. 14 is 28% of __50__

8. 97 is 82% of __118.3__

9. 27 is 300% of __9__

10. 63 is 50% of __126__

11. 19 is 100% of __19__

12. 15 is 47% of __32__

13. 37 is 40% of __92.5__

14. 75 is 200% of __37.5__

Total Problems __14__ Problems Correct ____

69

Name_____   Skill: Finding Percentages

Solve. Round to the nearest tenth.

1. 30 is 45% of __66.6__

2. 22 is 80% of __27.5__

3. 40 is 20% of __200__

4. 42 is 50% of __84__

5. 6 is 40% of __15__

6. 10 is 90% of __11.1__

7. 12 is 30% of __40__

8. 95 is 80% of __118.8__

9. 48 is 4% of __1,200__

10. 4 is 48% of __8.3__

11. 6 is 3% of __200__

12. 16 is 28% of __57.1__

13. 87 is 10% of __870__

14. 9 is 50% of __18__

Total Problems __14__ Problems Correct ____

70

Name_____   Skill: Finding Percentages

Solve.

1. __126__ is 90% of 140

2. __12__ is 200% of 6

3. __48__ is 40% of 120

4. __64.6__ is 68% of 95

5. __63__ is 70% of 90

6. __37.5__ is 25% of 150

7. __58.5__ is 45% of 130

8. __8.25__ is 55% of 15

9. __103.5__ is 75% of 138

10. __13.5__ is 15% of 90

11. __14.16__ is 12% of 118

12. __61.04__ is 28% of 218

13. __55.1__ is 19% of 290

14. __196__ is 35% of 560

Total Problems __14__ Problems Correct ____

71

Name_____   Skill: Finding Percentages

Solve.

1. __7__ is 14% of 50

2. __17.85__ is 21% of 85

3. __32.56__ is 37% of 88

4. __24__ is 32% of 75

5. __15.6__ is 52% of 30

6. __51.15__ is 55% of 93

7. __38.4__ is 48% of 80

8. __12.42__ is 23% of 54

9. __9.9__ is 18% of 55

10. __28.86__ is 74% of 39

11. __15.2__ is 16% of 95

12. __27__ is 45% of 60

13. __23.52__ is 24% of 98

14. __24.5__ is 35% of 70

Total Problems __14__ Problems Correct ____

72

Answer Key

Name_____   Skill: Calculating Interest

Calculate the amount of interest for the following. Round to the nearest cent. Use the formula, **Interest = Principal x rate x time**.

	Principal	Rate	Time	Interest
1.	$400.00	8%	1 year	$32.00
2.	$300.00	4%	1 year	$12.00
3.	$150.00	15%	2 years	$45.00
4.	$75.00	4%	4 years	$12.00
5.	$800.00	25%	3 years	$600.00
6.	$35.50	16%	3 years	$17.04
7.	$22.45	9%	2 years	$4.04
8.	$239.00	18%	1 year	$43.02
9.	$16.00	3%	5 years	$2.40
10.	$573.00	7%	7 years	$280.77

Total Problems _10_ Problems Correct ____

73

Name_____   Skill: Calculating Interest

Calculate the amount of interest for the following. Round to the nearest cent. Use the formula, **Interest = Principal x rate x time**.

	Principal	Rate	Time	Interest
1.	$42.50	20%	4 years	$34.00
2.	$135.25	4.8%	8 years	$51.94
3.	$874.00	9%	2 years	$157.32
4.	$502.00	5.25%	3 years	$79.07
5.	$139.00	16.4%	7 years	$159.57
6.	$287.35	8.5%	1 year	$24.42
7.	$495.50	36%	2 years	$356.76
8.	$1,397.00	6.5%	5 years	$454.03
9.	$428.78	5.42%	3 years	$69.72
10.	$309.53	8.7%	4 years	$107.72

Total Problems _10_ Problems Correct ____

74

Name_____   Skill: Lines, Line Segments, and Rays

Name the following lines, line segments, or rays.

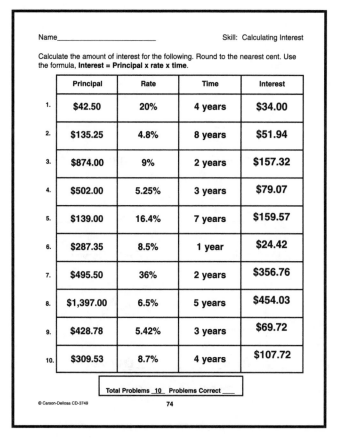

1. _____ **Line EF**

2. _____ **Ray IJ**

3. _____ **Line Segment MN**

4. _____ **Line ST**

5. _____ **Line Segment AB**

6. _____ **Ray KL**

7. _____ **Line QR**

8. _____ **Line CD**

Total Problems _8_ Problems Correct ____

75

Name_____   Skill: Naming Parallel and Intersecting Lines

Tell whether the following lines are parallel, intersecting, or perpendicular.

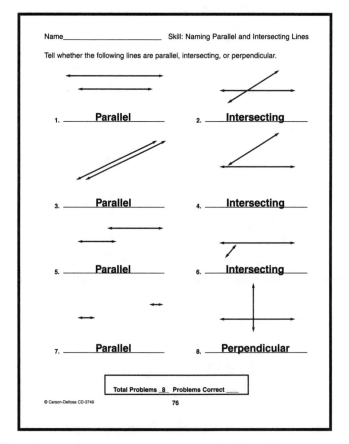

1. _____ **Parallel**

2. _____ **Intersecting**

3. _____ **Parallel**

4. _____ **Intersecting**

5. _____ **Parallel**

6. _____ **Intersecting**

7. _____ **Parallel**

8. _____ **Perpendicular**

Total Problems _8_ Problems Correct ____

76

Answer Key

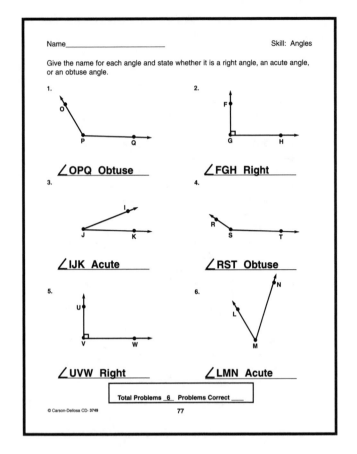

77

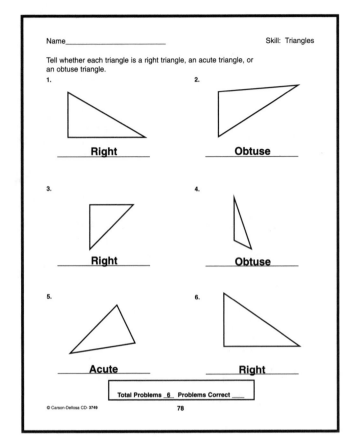

78

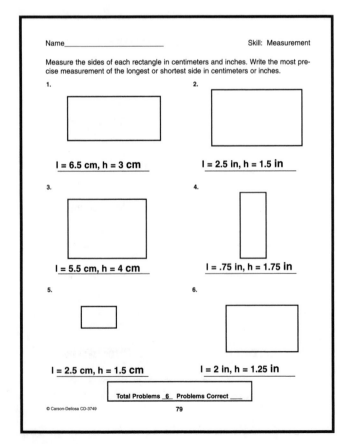

79

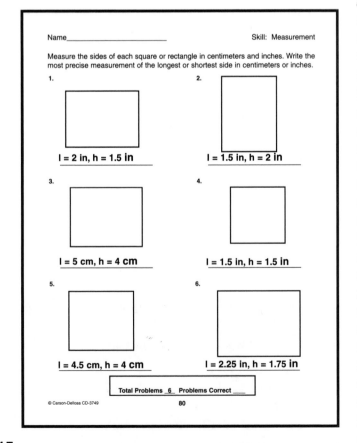

80

Answer Key

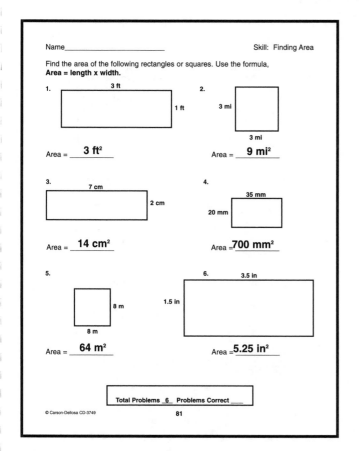

Name_____   Skill: Finding Area

Find the area of the following rectangles or squares. Use the formula,
Area = length x width.

1.   3 ft

Area = __**3 ft²**__

2.   3 mi / 3 mi

Area = __**9 mi²**__

3.   7 cm / 2 cm

Area = __**14 cm²**__

4.   35 mm / 20 mm

Area = __**700 mm²**__

5.   8 m / 8 m

Area = __**64 m²**__

6.   3.5 in / 1.5 in

Area = __**5.25 in²**__

Total Problems _6_ Problems Correct ____

© Carson-Dellosa CD-3749   81

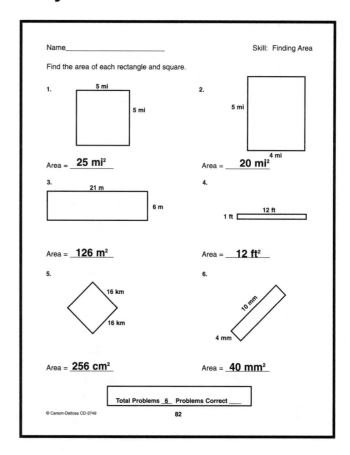

Name_____   Skill: Finding Area

Find the area of each rectangle and square.

1.   5 mi / 5 mi

Area = __**25 mi²**__

2.   5 mi / 4 mi

Area = __**20 mi²**__

3.   21 m / 6 m

Area = __**126 m²**__

4.   12 ft / 1 ft

Area = __**12 ft²**__

5.   16 km / 16 km

Area = __**256 cm²**__

6.   10 mm / 4 mm

Area = __**40 mm²**__

Total Problems _6_ Problems Correct ____

© Carson-Dellosa CD-3749   82

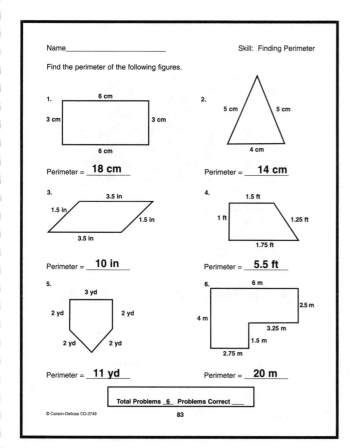

Name_____   Skill: Finding Perimeter

Find the perimeter of the following figures.

1.   6 cm / 3 cm / 3 cm / 6 cm

Perimeter = __**18 cm**__

2.   5 cm / 5 cm / 4 cm

Perimeter = __**14 cm**__

3.   3.5 in / 1.5 in / 1.5 in / 3.5 in

Perimeter = __**10 in**__

4.   1.5 ft / 1 ft / 1.25 ft / 1.75 ft

Perimeter = __**5.5 ft**__

5.   3 yd / 2 yd / 2 yd / 2 yd / 2 yd

Perimeter = __**11 yd**__

6.   6 m / 2.5 m / 3.25 m / 1.5 m / 2.75 m / 4 m

Perimeter = __**20 m**__

Total Problems _6_ Problems Correct ____

© Carson-Dellosa CD-3749   83

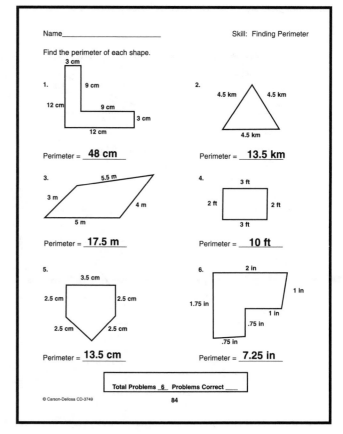

Name_____   Skill: Finding Perimeter

Find the perimeter of each shape.

1.   3 cm / 9 cm / 12 cm / 9 cm / 3 cm / 12 cm

Perimeter = __**48 cm**__

2.   4.5 km / 4.5 km / 4.5 km

Perimeter = __**13.5 km**__

3.   5.5 m / 3 m / 4 m / 5 m

Perimeter = __**17.5 m**__

4.   3 ft / 2 ft / 2 ft / 3 ft

Perimeter = __**10 ft**__

5.   3.5 cm / 2.5 cm / 2.5 cm / 2.5 cm / 2.5 cm

Perimeter = __**13.5 cm**__

6.   2 in / 1 in / 1 in / .75 in / .75 in / 1.75 in

Perimeter = __**7.25 in**__

Total Problems _6_ Problems Correct ____

© Carson-Dellosa CD-3749   84

© Carson-Dellosa CD-3749   116

Answer Key

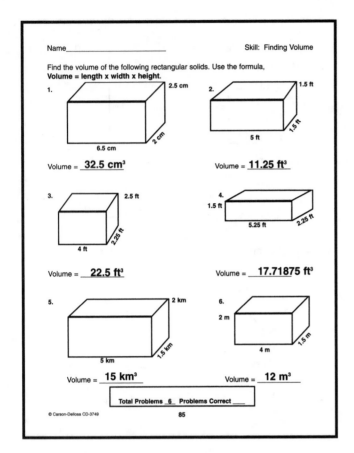

Name_____   Skill: Finding Volume

Find the volume of the following rectangular solids. Use the formula,
Volume = length x width x height.

1.
2.5 cm, 6.5 cm, 2 cm
Volume = **32.5 cm³**

2.
1.5 ft, 5 ft, 1.5 ft
Volume = **11.25 ft³**

3.
2.5 ft, 4 ft, 2.25 ft
Volume = **22.5 ft³**

4.
1.5 ft, 5.25 ft, 2.25 ft
Volume = **17.71875 ft³**

5.
2 km, 5 km, 1.5 km
Volume = **15 km³**

6.
2 m, 4 m, 1.5 m
Volume = **12 m³**

Total Problems _6_ Problems Correct ____

© Carson-Dellosa CD-3749   85

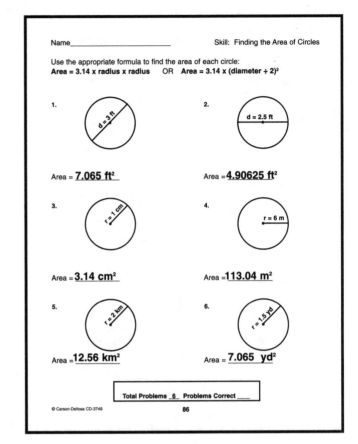

Name_____   Skill: Finding the Area of Circles

Use the appropriate formula to find the area of each circle:
Area = 3.14 x radius x radius   OR   Area = 3.14 x (diameter ÷ 2)²

1. d = 3 ft
Area = **7.065 ft²**

2. d = 2.5 ft
Area = **4.90625 ft²**

3. r = 1 cm
Area = **3.14 cm²**

4. r = 6 m
Area = **113.04 m²**

5. r = 2 km
Area = **12.56 km²**

6. r = 1.5 yd
Area = **7.065 yd²**

Total Problems _6_ Problems Correct ____

© Carson-Dellosa CD-3749   86

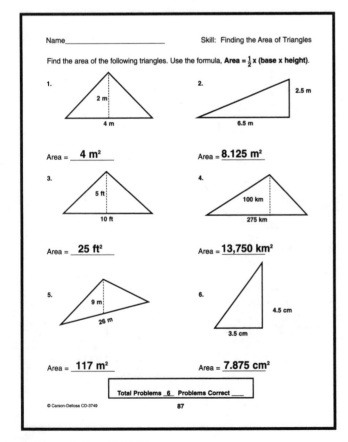

Name_____   Skill: Finding the Area of Triangles

Find the area of the following triangles. Use the formula, **Area = ½ x (base x height)**.

1.
2 m, 4 m
Area = **4 m²**

2.
2.5 m, 6.5 m
Area = **8.125 m²**

3.
5 ft, 10 ft
Area = **25 ft²**

4.
100 km, 275 km
Area = **13,750 km²**

5.
9 m, 26 m
Area = **117 m²**

6.
4.5 cm, 3.5 cm
Area = **7.875 cm²**

Total Problems _6_ Problems Correct ____

© Carson-Dellosa CD-3749   87

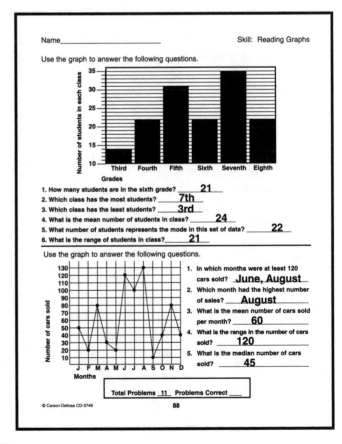

Name_____   Skill: Reading Graphs

Use the graph to answer the following questions.

1. How many students are in the sixth grade? ____ **21** ____
2. Which class has the most students? ____ **7th** ____
3. Which class has the least students? ____ **3rd** ____
4. What is the mean number of students in class? ____ **24** ____
5. What number of students represents the mode in this set of data? ____ **22** ____
6. What is the range of students in class? ____ **21** ____

Use the graph to answer the following questions.

1. In which months were at least 120 cars sold? **June, August**
2. Which month had the highest number of sales? **August**
3. What is the mean number of cars sold per month? **60**
4. What is the range in the number of cars sold? **120**
5. What is the median number of cars sold? **45**

Total Problems _11_ Problems Correct ____

© Carson-Dellosa CD-3749   88

© Carson-Dellosa CD-3749   **117**

Answer Key

Page 89

Name_____   Skill: Identifying Points on a Graph

Identify the points.

1. A (_8_ , _9_)
2. B (_2_ , _8_)
3. C (_6_ , _8_)
4. D (_7_ , _2_)
5. E (_1_ , _4_)
6. F (_3_ , _4_)
7. G (_6_ , _6_)
8. H (_1_ , _2_)
9. I (_5_ , _3_)
10. J (_10_ , _6_)

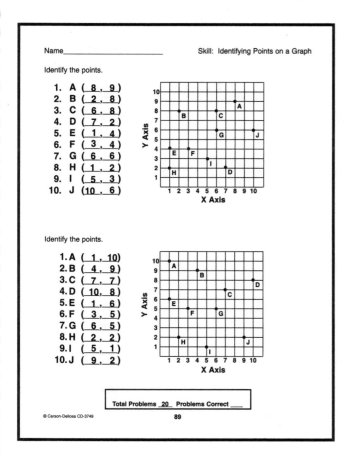

Identify the points.

1. A (_1_ , _10_)
2. B (_4_ , _9_)
3. C (_7_ , _7_)
4. D (_10_ , _8_)
5. E (_1_ , _6_)
6. F (_3_ , _5_)
7. G (_6_ , _5_)
8. H (_2_ , _2_)
9. I (_5_ , _1_)
10. J (_9_ , _2_)

Total Problems _20_ Problems Correct ____

© Carson-Dellosa CD-3749

89

Page 90

Name_____   Skill: Creating Line Graphs

Use the following information to make a line graph. First, title the graph. Next, name the X axis *Months* and the Y axis *Number of Students*, and label the graph. Finally, plot the data.

Number of students on the honor roll per month.

Month	
January	13
February	20
March	17
April	25
May	12
September	15
October	14
November	21
December	25

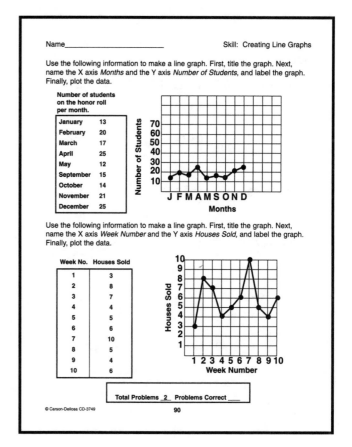

Use the following information to make a line graph. First, title the graph. Next, name the X axis *Week Number* and the Y axis *Houses Sold,* and label the graph. Finally, plot the data.

Week No.	Houses Sold
1	3
2	8
3	7
4	4
5	5
6	6
7	10
8	5
9	4
10	6

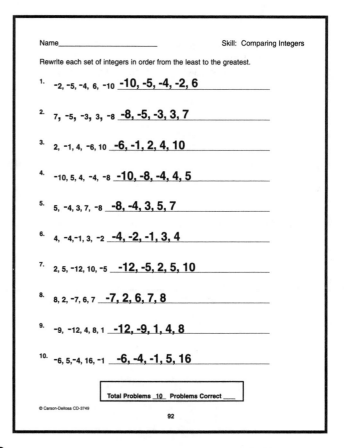

Total Problems _2_ Problems Correct ____

© Carson-Dellosa CD-3749

90

Page 91

Name_____   Skill: Comparing Integers

Fill in the circle with <, >, or = to make each statement true.

1. 2 ⊃ -2
2. -5 ⊃ -7
3. -1 ⊂ 1
4. 4 ⊃ -3

5. -6 ⊃ -10
6. -6 ⊃ -9
7. -1 ⊂ 2
8. -6 ⊂ 3

9. -3 ⊂ 1
10. -2 ⊂ 0
11. 5 ⊃ 0
12. -6 ⊂ 5

13. -3 ⊃ -9
14. 9 ⊃ -2
15. 4 ⊃ -2
16. -3 ⊃ -5

Total Problems _16_ Problems Correct ____

© Carson-Dellosa CD-3749

91

Page 92

Name_____   Skill: Comparing Integers

Rewrite each set of integers in order from the least to the greatest.

1. -2, -5, -4, 6, -10   **-10, -5, -4, -2, 6**

2. 7, -5, -3, 3, -8   **-8, -5, -3, 3, 7**

3. 2, -1, 4, -6, 10   **-6, -1, 2, 4, 10**

4. -10, 5, 4, -4, -8   **-10, -8, -4, 4, 5**

5. 5, -4, 3, 7, -8   **-8, -4, 3, 5, 7**

6. 4, -4, -1, 3, -2   **-4, -2, -1, 3, 4**

7. 2, 5, -12, 10, -5   **-12, -5, 2, 5, 10**

8. 8, 2, -7, 6, 7   **-7, 2, 6, 7, 8**

9. -9, -12, 4, 8, 1   **-12, -9, 1, 4, 8**

10. -6, 5, -4, 16, -1   **-6, -4, -1, 5, 16**

Total Problems _10_ Problems Correct ____

© Carson-Dellosa CD-3749

92

Answer Key

Name_____   Skill: Adding and Subtracting Integers

Add or subtract.

1. $^-3 + ^-5 = ^-2$

2. $^-4 + ^-2 = ^-6$

3. $^-6 + 4 = ^-2$

4. $10 + ^-10 = 0$

5. $^-6 + 3 = ^-3$

6. $^-4 + ^-8 = ^-12$

7. $^-1 + ^-8 = ^-9$

8. $5 + 6 = 11$

9. $^-9 + ^-8 = 1$

10. $4 - ^-3 = 7$

11. $^-4 - ^-5 = 1$

12. $^-9 - 5 = ^-14$

13. $10 - ^-11 = 21$

14. $^-8 - 8 = ^-16$

15. $^-2 - ^-4 = 2$

16. $^-7 - ^-8 = 1$

17. $5 - 6 = -1$

18. $6 - ^-8 = 14$

Total Problems 18 Problems Correct ____

93

Name_____   Skill: Finding Exponents

Solve using a calculator.

1. $10^9 = $ 1,000,000,000

2. $8^6 = 262,144$

3. $7^9 = $ 40,353,607

4. $4^6 = 4,096$

5. $9^8 = $ 43,046,721

6. $10^7 = $ 10,000,000

7. $6^5 = 7,776$

8. $5^7 = 78,125$

9. $3^8 = 6,561$

10. $2^{10} = 1,024$

11. $8^5 = 32,768$

12. $9^3 = 729$

13. $3^9 = 19,683$

14. $1^{10} = 1$

15. $7^4 = 2,401$

16. $5^3 = 125$

Total Problems 16 Problems Correct ____

94

Name_____   Skill: Finding Exponents

Solve without using a calculator.

1. $1^5 = 1$

2. $6^2 = 36$

3. $10^3 = 1,000$

4. $3^2 = 9$

5. $4^4 = 256$

6. $7^2 = 49$

7. $2^4 = 16$

8. $5^5 = 3,125$

9. $8^2 = 64$

10. $9^4 = 6,561$

11. $10^8 = $ 100,000,000

12. $3^5 = 243$

13. $7^3 = 343$

14. $2^9 = 512$

15. $6^4 = 1,296$

16. $8^3 = 512$

Total Problems 16 Problems Correct ____

95

Add.

$$\begin{array}{r} 2{,}336 \\ +\ \ \ 54 \\ \hline \end{array}$$

Add.

$$\begin{array}{r} 4{,}870 \\ +\ 285 \\ \hline \end{array}$$

Add.

$$\begin{array}{r} 202 \\ 125 \\ +\ 682 \\ \hline \end{array}$$

Add.

$$\begin{array}{r} 9{,}210 \\ 125 \\ +\ \ \ 42 \\ \hline \end{array}$$

Subtract.

$$\begin{array}{r} 88 \\ -\ 27 \\ \hline \end{array}$$

Subtract.

$$\begin{array}{r} 95 \\ -\ 87 \\ \hline \end{array}$$

Subtract.

$$\begin{array}{r} 488 \\ -\ 243 \\ \hline \end{array}$$

Subtract.

$$\begin{array}{r} 31{,}621 \\ -\ 23{,}126 \\ \hline \end{array}$$

Multiply.

$$\begin{array}{r} 320 \\ \times\ 7 \\ \hline \end{array}$$

Multiply.

$$\begin{array}{r} 2{,}587 \\ \times\ \ 24 \\ \hline \end{array}$$

Multiply.

$$\begin{array}{r} 625 \\ \times\ 17 \\ \hline \end{array}$$

Multiply.

$$\begin{array}{r} 370 \\ \times\ 239 \\ \hline \end{array}$$

Divide.

$$9\,\overline{)2{,}790}$$

Divide.

$$3\,\overline{)627}$$

Divide.

$$45\,\overline{)990}$$

Divide.

$$56\,\overline{)647}$$

9,377

8,495

88,430

11 r31

1,009

245

10,625

22

5,155

8

62,088

209

2,390

61

2,240

310

Change to simplest form.

$$\frac{6}{8}$$

Change to a fraction.

$$12\frac{13}{15}$$

Change to a mixed number.

$$\frac{4}{3}$$

Make the fractions equivalent.

$$\frac{2}{3} = \frac{}{12}$$

Change to simplest form.

$$\frac{5}{25}$$

Change to a fraction.

$$2\frac{3}{8}$$

Change to a mixed number.

$$\frac{8}{3}$$

Make the fractions equivalent.

$$\frac{3}{7} = \frac{}{14}$$

Change to simplest form.

$$\frac{15}{30}$$

Change to a fraction.

$$6\frac{1}{5}$$

Change to a mixed number.

$$\frac{13}{4}$$

Divide.

$$\frac{9}{16} \div \frac{3}{4}$$

Change to simplest form.

$$\frac{24}{32}$$

Change to a fraction.

$$8\frac{2}{3}$$

Change to a mixed number.

$$\frac{43}{7}$$

Divide.

$$\frac{4}{9} \div \frac{3}{4}$$

$\frac{16}{27}$	$6\frac{1}{7}$	$\frac{26}{3}$	$\frac{3}{4}$
$\frac{3}{4}$	$3\frac{1}{4}$	$\frac{31}{5}$	$\frac{1}{2}$
6	$2\frac{2}{3}$	$\frac{19}{8}$	$\frac{1}{5}$
8	$1\frac{1}{3}$	$\frac{193}{15}$	$\frac{3}{4}$

Multiply.

$$6\frac{7}{8} \times 3\frac{1}{3} =$$

Add.

$$\frac{1}{2} + \frac{1}{2} =$$

Add.

$$6\frac{3}{10} + 7\frac{1}{3} =$$

Subtract.

$$8\frac{4}{5} - 2\frac{1}{5} =$$

Multiply.

$$3\frac{1}{2} \times 4 =$$

Add.

$$\frac{3}{8} + \frac{1}{8} =$$

Add.

$$\frac{2}{9} + \frac{2}{3} =$$

Subtract.

$$4 - \frac{2}{3} =$$

Multiply.

$$\frac{3}{9} \times 4 =$$

Multiply.

$$\frac{5}{6} \times 5 =$$

Add.

$$\frac{1}{10} + \frac{4}{8} =$$

Subtract.

$$\frac{5}{7} - \frac{2}{7} =$$

Multiply.

$$\frac{3}{4} \times \frac{2}{3} =$$

Multiply.

$$\frac{3}{5} \times \frac{1}{2} =$$

Add.

$$1\frac{2}{5} + 2\frac{3}{5} =$$

Subtract.

$$\frac{9}{14} - \frac{1}{14} =$$

$22\frac{11}{12}$

1

$13\frac{19}{30}$

$6\frac{3}{5}$

14

$\frac{1}{2}$

$\frac{8}{9}$

$3\frac{1}{3}$

$1\frac{1}{3}$

$4\frac{1}{6}$

$\frac{3}{5}$

$\frac{3}{7}$

$\frac{1}{2}$

$\frac{3}{10}$

4

$\frac{4}{7}$

Subtract.

$2\frac{1}{6} - 1\frac{5}{6} =$

Subtract

$5\frac{2}{3} - 3\frac{1}{4} =$

Add.

$$\begin{array}{r} .603 \\ + 1.7 \\ \hline \end{array}$$

Add.

$$\begin{array}{r} 14.2 \\ + 16.5 \\ \hline \end{array}$$

Add.

$13.87 + 16.1 =$

Add.

$.52 + 123.4 =$

Subtract.

$$\begin{array}{r} 306.45 \\ - 11.5 \\ \hline \end{array}$$

Subtract.

$$\begin{array}{r} 75.4 \\ - 3.2 \\ \hline \end{array}$$

Subtract.

$28.4 - 4.62 =$

Subtract.

$42.619 - 7.3 =$

Multiply.

$$\begin{array}{r} 4.44 \\ \times\ .67 \\ \hline \end{array}$$

Multiply.

$$\begin{array}{r} 6.4 \\ \times\ 2.5 \\ \hline \end{array}$$

Multiply.

$87.1 \times .25 =$

Multiply.

$9.5 \times 260.4 =$

Divide.

$5\overline{)\,.865}$

Divide.

$6\overline{)\,3.6}$

2.303

294.95

2.9748

.173

30.7

72.2

16

.6

$2\frac{5}{12}$

123.92

35.319

2,473.8

$\frac{1}{3}$

29.97

23.78

21.775

Divide.

$35.6 \div 2 =$

Divide.

$82.16 \div 15.8 =$

Change to a fraction.

.8

Change to a fraction.

.68

Change to a fraction.

6.5

Change to a decimal.

75.2

Change to a decimal.

$\frac{5}{8}$

Change to a decimal.

$\frac{11}{20}$

Change to a fraction.

80%

Change to a fraction.

15%

Change to a fraction.

85%

Change to a fraction.

20%

Change to a percent.

$\frac{2}{5}$

Change to a percent.

$\frac{7}{20}$

Change to a percent.

$4 \frac{5}{25}$

Change to a percent.

$5 \frac{10}{50}$

$\dfrac{17}{25}$

.55

$\dfrac{1}{5}$

520%

$\dfrac{4}{5}$

.625

$\dfrac{17}{20}$

420%

5.2

$75\dfrac{1}{5}$

$\dfrac{3}{20}$

35%

17.8

$6\dfrac{1}{2}$

$\dfrac{4}{5}$

40%

Solve.

5% of 80 = _____

© CD-3749

Solve.

16% of 110 = _____

© CD-3749

Solve.

45% of 30 = _____

© CD-3749

Solve.

15% of 60 = _____

© CD-3749

Calculate the interest.

**Principal = $400.00
Rate = 5%
Time = 2 years**

© CD-3749

Calculate the interest.

**Principal = $150.00
Rate = 6%
Time = 3 years**

© CD-3749

Identify the type of angle as: right, obtuse, or acute.

© CD-3749

Identify the type of angle as: right, obtuse, or acute.

© CD-3749

Solve.

9^2

© CD-3749

Solve.

10^6

© CD-3749

Identify the type of triangle as: right, obtuse, or acute.

© CD-3749

Identify the type of triangle as: right, obtuse, or acute.

© CD-3749

Find the perimeter.

7 m   4 m   7 m

© CD-3749

Find the perimeter.

3 ft   2 ft   3 ft   2 ft

© CD-3749

Find the area.

4 cm   4 cm

© CD-3749

Find the area.

6 mi   1 mi

© CD-3749

9

13.5

17.6

4

Acute Angle

Right Angle

$27.00

$40.00

Obtuse Triangle

Right Triangle

1,000,000

81

6 mi²

16 cm²

10 ft

22 m